I am overwhelmed with gratitude as I reflect on the incredible journey of bringing "Transforming Project Managers to Agile Roles" to life. It wouldn't have been possible without the unwavering support and encouragement from a remarkable group of individuals.

To my cherished family, your boundless love and understanding sustained me through this journey. Your belief in my vision kept me inspired, and I am profoundly grateful for the sacrifices you made for me to see my dreams come true. To my dear friends and well-wishers, your words of encouragement were the fuel that powered me through the challenges. Your enthusiasm for this endeavor lifted my spirits and reminded me of the importance of community and shared dreams.

To the Agile and Management Gurus whose wisdom has shaped my thinking, your teachings have been a guiding light throughout this writing process and enriched the content of this book.

With gratitude for the unwavering support of family, friends, and mentors who have been pillars of strength throughout this writing odyssey. Your encouragement has been the wind beneath my wings.

As my book "Transforming Project Managers to Agile Roles" embarks on its journey into the hands of readers, it carries my gratitude for the role you played in bringing this vision to life. Thank you for being a part of this significant chapter in my life.

With heartfelt appreciation,

K.Chakravarthy

TRANSFORMING PROJECT MANAGERS TO AGILE ROLES

GUIDING 21ST CENTURY MANAGERS, LEADERS & ORGANIZATIONS

K.CHAKRAVARTHY

Contents

Contents

About Author

"Katuru Kalyan Chakravarthy", a Technology Program and Product Management Leader with extensive experience in Agile Leadership, Applications Design, Development, Quality Engineering, and Automation. He has consistently demonstrated exemplary leadership skills, driving successful Enterprise Agile Transformations and playing a pivotal role in coaching and leading numerous teams. His contributions to the field of Agile are not only reflected in his practical experience but also in his insightful publications on LinkedIn which influenced thousands of professionals across the globe.

He was also a Test Automation Architect, with a rich background in Automation Frameworks Design, Development, and Maintenance. What sets him apart is not just his technical prowess but also his commitment to knowledge sharing. With achievements like publishing rich content on LinkedIn and guided thousands of Test Engineers through articles like "Be an Automation Tester by 2020.. Why & How," he has had a lasting impact on the Testing Community also.

In addition to his professional accomplishments, He has shown a commitment to continuous learning, as evidenced by his extensive professional education. Accomplished Professional Specializations in Azure Data Science, AI Product Management, Google Cloud Digital Leadership, Executive Data Science, Agile Leadership, etc. offered by the reputable institutions through Coursera. He has pursued his B.Tech in Computer Science Engineering from JNTU and also accomplished MicroMasters Programs in Business Management and Entrepreneurship from IIM Bangalore through edx.

Author's e-mail id: engineer.kalyan@gmail.com

Disclaimer

This book is a culmination of author's extensive experience and expertise in the field, supplemented by insights gathered from diverse sources such as articles, blogs, books, white papers, AI models, courses, videos, professional education programs, certifications and more. While every effort has been made to ensure accuracy and reliability, the content reflects a synthesis of knowledge rather than direct replication of specific sources. The intention is to provide a comprehensive and informed perspective on the subject matter. Readers are encouraged to consult additional references and conduct further research to enhance their understanding. The author disclaim any liability arising directly or indirectly from the use of the information presented in this book.

Preface

In the dynamic landscape of contemporary business, the shift from traditional project management methodologies to Agile practices has become more than a mere trend—it is a transformative journey that shapes the very fabric of organizational success. This book "Transforming Project Managers to Agile Roles" is a culmination of my experiences, insights, and learnings as I navigated the intricate path from conventional project management to the agility demanded by today's organizations.

It is not merely a guide but an invitation to the managers and leaders to embark on a transformative journey, one that expands their horizons and positions them at the forefront of organizational innovation. In the pages that follow, we will delve into the principles and practices of Agile Management, unraveling its intricacies and highlighting the reasons why this shift is no longer an option but a strategic imperative. We will explore how traditional project managers can seamlessly transition into new roles such as Agile Practitioners, Scrum Masters, and Product Owners, unlocking doors to exciting opportunities in the ever-evolving field of Agile Management.

Through this exploration, I aim to provide a roadmap for traditional project managers to thrive in the era of Agile Transformation. As we embark on this journey together, I invite you to embrace the transformative power of Agile Management. The future of project management is agile, and it is my sincere hope that this book serves as a compass for those navigating the exciting terrain of Agile Transformation.

Thank you,
K.Chakravarthy

Management- A Historical Perspective

Management, as a concept, has undergone a remarkable evolution throughout history. From its humble beginnings in ancient civilizations to the sophisticated organizational structures of the modern era, the history of management reflects the dynamic and ever-changing nature of human endeavors. In this chapter, we will trace the development of management in organizations, highlighting key milestones and influential theories that have shaped the way businesses are run today.

Ancient Management Practices:

The roots of management can be traced back to ancient civilizations where basic organizational structures and hierarchies began to emerge. Ancient management history is a fascinating exploration of organizational principles and leadership practices that evolved in civilizations long gone. In ancient Egypt, for example, the construction of monumental structures such as the pyramids required coordination and organization. Ancient Greece contributed to management thought through the works of philosophers like Aristotle, who explored the concept of virtuous leadership. The Roman Empire further advanced organizational structures, introducing hierarchical systems and principles of governance that influenced management practices for centuries. These ancient management histories collectively laid the groundwork for the principles and philosophies that continue to shape modern organizational management. Studying the roots of management in ancient civilizations provides valuable insights into the timeless principles of effective leadership and organizational dynamics.

Chanakya's Management:

Chanakya, also known as Kautilya or Vishnugupta, was an ancient Indian philosopher, teacher, economist, jurist, and royal advisor who lived during the 4th century BCE. He is best known for his seminal work, the Arthashastra, an ancient Indian treatise on statecraft, economic policy, and military strategy. While primarily focused on governance, the Arthashastra contains invaluable insights into effective management principles that are still relevant today.

Chanakya's management philosophy emphasizes the importance of strategic planning, efficient resource allocation, and ethical leadership. His teachings highlight the significance of understanding human nature, fostering teamwork, and adapting strategies to changing circumstances. Chanakya's emphasis on diplomacy, intelligence gathering, and maintaining a strong and disciplined administration reflects his keen understanding of the complexities of leadership and governance. His enduring influence is evident in the continued study and application of his principles in contemporary management literature and leadership development programs. Chanakya's timeless wisdom continues to inspire leaders worldwide, making him a revered figure in the management history.

Scientific Management:

The late 19th and early 20th centuries saw the emergence of scientific management, championed by Frederick W. Taylor. Taylor's principles focused on optimizing efficiency in manufacturing processes through systematic observation, measurement, and analysis. His work laid the foundation for the development of standardized work procedures and the concept of time and motion studies.

Administrative Management:

Around the same time, Henri Fayol, a French mining engineer, introduced administrative management principles. Fayol's work emphasized the importance of organizational structure, coordination, and managerial functions. He proposed the classic principles of management, including unity of command, scalar chain, and division of work, which are still relevant in contemporary organizational management.

Human Relations Movement:

As industrialization progressed, the focus shifted from efficiency to the human side of organizations. The Human Relations Movement, led by Elton Mayo and others, emphasized the importance of understanding and addressing the social and psychological needs of employees. This perspective marked a significant departure from the mechanistic views of the management.

Systems Theory and Contingency Management:

In the mid-20th century, management theorists began to explore organizations as complex systems. The systems theory, developed by scholars like Ludwig von Bertalanffy, emphasized the interdependence of various organizational components. Additionally, contingency management theories, such as those proposed by Peter Drucker, acknowledged that management practices should be contingent upon the unique characteristics of each organization.

Total Quality Management (TQM) and Continuous Improvement:

In the latter half of the 20th century, a shift towards quality and continuous improvement gained prominence. Total Quality Management, popularized by thinkers like W. Edwards Deming and Joseph Juran, focused on customer satisfaction, employee involvement, and continuous process improvement. This era marked a transition from a command-and-control approach to a more participative and collaborative management style.

Contemporary Management Theories:

In the 21st century, management continues to evolve with the rise of technology, globalization, and changing societal expectations. Contemporary management theories, including agile management, lean management, and strategic management, reflect the need for adaptability and responsiveness in the face of rapid change.

Summary

The history of management in organizations is a rich tapestry woven with diverse influences, theories, and practices. From the rudimentary organizational structures of ancient civilizations to the sophisticated and dynamic management systems of today, the journey of management has been one of adaptation and innovation. As we continue to navigate the complexities of the modern business landscape, an understanding of the historical evolution of management provides valuable insights for shaping the future of organizational leadership and governance.

Demystifying Value Driven Delivery

In the ever-evolving landscape of project management and product development, the pursuit of value has become a guiding principle for successful and impactful endeavors. Value-driven delivery represents an approach that places a paramount focus on delivering tangible value to stakeholders and customers. This chapter explores the concept of value-driven delivery, outlining its principles, methodologies, and the profound impact it has on project success.

Defining Value-Driven Delivery:

Value-driven delivery is a project management and product development approach that prioritizes the delivery of valuable outcomes over strict adherence to predefined plans or processes. At its core, this approach recognizes that value is not only about meeting project requirements but also about fulfilling the needs and expectations of stakeholders and end-users. Value-driven delivery is closely associated with agile methodologies and principles, emphasizing adaptability, customer collaboration, and the ability to respond to change. Key principles, methodologies and benefits of Value Driven Delivery are discussed in the following sections.

Key Principles of Value-Driven Delivery:

- **Customer-Centricity:** The primary focus of value-driven delivery is on satisfying the needs and expectations tof customers. Understanding and prioritizing customer requirements and feedback are central to the decision-making process.

- **Adaptability:** Value-driven delivery embraces change as a natural part of the development process. It prioritizes adaptability over rigid adherence to plans, allowing teams to respond to evolving customer needs and market dynamics.

- **Incremental and Iterative Development:** Rather than aiming for a single, comprehensive release, value-driven delivery encourages incremental and iterative development. This approach enables the delivery of smaller, valuable increments of work that can be quickly deployed and tested.

- **Continuous Feedback:** Frequent and continuous feedback loops are integral to value-driven delivery. Regular interactions with stakeholders and end-users provide valuable insights, allowing teams to make informed decisions and adjustments throughout the development lifecycle.

- **Measurable Outcomes:** Value-driven delivery emphasizes the importance of defining and measuring outcomes. Teams establish clear metrics to assess the success of a project or product, ensuring that delivered features contribute meaningfully to the overall value proposition.

- **Collaboration and Communication:** Effective collaboration and communication are key principles of value-driven delivery. Transparent communication between team members, stakeholders, and customers fosters a shared understanding of goals and priorities.

Methodologies and Frameworks Associated with Value-Driven Delivery:

- **Agile Methodologies:** Agile methodologies, including Scrum and Kanban, are closely aligned with value-driven delivery principles. These frameworks emphasize iterative development, collaboration, and a customer-centric approach to delivering value.

- **Lean Thinking:** Lean thinking, inspired by principles from lean manufacturing, is focused on delivering value with the least amount of waste. It complements value-driven delivery by encouraging the elimination of unnecessary processes and maximizing the delivery of customer value.

- **DevOps:** DevOps practices, which aim to integrate development and operations seamlessly, contribute to value-driven delivery by automating processes, reducing deployment times, and enhancing overall product quality.

- **Design Thinking:** Design thinking, with its emphasis on empathetic understanding and iterative prototyping, aligns with value-driven delivery by ensuring that products are not only functional but also meet the emotional and experiential needs of users.

Benefits of Value-Driven Delivery:

- **Customer Satisfaction:** By prioritizing customer needs and incorporating continuous feedback, value-driven delivery enhances customer satisfaction. Products and projects are more likely to meet or exceed customer expectations.

- **Adaptability to Change:** The adaptability inherent in value-driven delivery allows teams to respond effectively to changing requirements, market conditions, and unforeseen challenges, ensuring that the delivered value remains relevant.

- **Faster Time-to-Market:** Incremental and iterative development, a hallmark of value-driven delivery, enables faster time-to-market. Delivering smaller increments of value allows organizations to respond quickly to market demands and gain a competitive edge.

- **Maximized ROI:** Value-driven delivery focuses on maximizing return on investment by ensuring that resources are allocated to features and improvements that deliver the most significant value to stakeholders and end-users.

- **Continuous Improvement:** The emphasis on measurable outcomes and feedback loops promotes a culture of continuous improvement. Teams are empowered to learn from each iteration and make data-driven decisions to enhance future deliveries.

Challenges of Value-Driven Delivery:

- **Cultural Resistance:** Implementing a value-driven approach may face resistance in organizations accustomed to more traditional, plan-driven methodologies. A cultural shift may be necessary to embrace the principles of value-driven delivery.

- **Data-Driven Decision-Making:** Value-driven delivery relies on data-driven decision-making, and organizations may face challenges in collecting and analyzing the necessary data to measure outcomes and prioritize features effectively.

- **Balancing Speed and Quality:** The desire for faster time-to-market should be balanced with maintaining product quality. Striking this balance requires careful consideration of testing, quality assurance, and release management practices.

Summary

Value-driven delivery represents a paradigm shift in project management and product development, placing value at the forefront of decision-making processes. By prioritizing customer satisfaction, embracing adaptability, and delivering measurable outcomes, organizations can not only meet the demands of a rapidly changing environment but also drive sustained success. As technology, markets, and customer expectations continue to evolve, the principles of value-driven delivery provide a guiding light for organizations seeking to navigate uncertainty and deliver meaningful and impactful outcomes.

CHAPTER THREE

Demystifying Empirical Process Control

Demystifying Empirical Process Control

In the dynamic landscape of project management and digital product development, where change is constant and unpredictability is the norm, traditional methods often fall short. Enter empirical process control, an approach that acknowledges the inherent unpredictability of complex systems and emphasizes continuous learning and adaptation. This chapter explores the concept of empirical process control, its principles, and how it is applied in various industries to manage projects and processes effectively.

Defining Empirical Process Control:

Empirical process control is a management and control approach that relies on observation, experimentation, and learning from experience to make informed decisions. It is based on the empirical foundation, which means that decisions are made based on evidence and real-world observations rather than relying solely on theoretical predictions or pre-defined plans. This approach recognizes the complexity and uncertainty inherent in many processes, encouraging adaptability and continuous improvement. Key principles, applications, benefits and challenges of empirical process control are discussed in following sections.

Key Principles of Empirical Process Control:

- **Transparency:** The first principle of empirical process control is transparency. All aspects of the process, including work progress, impediments, and decision-making, should be visible and accessible to all stakeholders. Transparency fosters open communication and shared understanding.

- **Inspection:** Inspection involves regularly assessing and evaluating the current state of the process or project. This includes examining work products, progress, and any issues that may arise. Inspection is a fundamental element in identifying opportunities for improvement.

- **Adaptation:** Adaptation is the core of empirical process control. Based on the observations and inspections, teams and organizations must be willing to adapt their processes, strategies, and plans. This continuous adaptation is essential for staying responsive to changing conditions.

- **Iteration:** The iterative nature of empirical process control emphasizes the need for frequent cycles of inspection and adaptation. This iterative approach allows for incremental improvements and ensures that the process remains aligned with project goals and evolving requirements.

Applying Empirical Process Control in Industries:

- **Agile Software Development:** Empirical process control is a foundational principle of agile methodologies, such as Scrum and Kanban. Agile teams regularly inspect and adapt their processes, responding to changing requirements and customer feedback to deliver valuable increments of work.

- **Project Management:** In project management, especially in industries like construction and manufacturing, empirical process control helps teams manage uncertainties and complexities. It enables project managers to adjust schedules, resource allocation, and project plans based on real-time information.

- **Quality Management:** Empirical process control is integral to quality management systems. By continuously inspecting and adapting processes, organizations can identify and address quality issues promptly, leading to improved products and services.

- **Product Development:** Product development teams use empirical process control to manage the intricacies of bringing a product from concept to market. This approach allows teams to iterate on product features, respond to user feedback, and make data-driven decisions.

Benefits of Empirical Process Control:

- **Flexibility:** Empirical process control provides the flexibility needed to adapt to changing conditions. This is particularly valuable in industries where requirements are volatile, and the ability to respond quickly is crucial.

- **Continuous Improvement:** The iterative nature of empirical process control promotes continuous improvement. Teams are encouraged to learn from each iteration, making adjustments to processes and practices for better outcomes in the future.

- **Risk Management:** By regularly inspecting and adapting, teams can identify and address potential risks early in the process. This proactive approach to risk management is essential for minimizing negative impacts on projects.

- **Customer Satisfaction:** In customer-centric industries, such as software development and product management, empirical process control contributes to higher customer satisfaction. The ability to respond to customer feedback and changing preferences ensures that the final product better aligns with user needs.

Challenges of Empirical Process Control:

- **Cultural Resistance:** Implementing empirical process control may face resistance in organizations accustomed to more traditional, plan-driven approaches. Shifting to an empirical mindset requires a cultural change and a commitment to continuous learning.

- **Data Availability:** Effective empirical process control relies on accurate and comprehensive data. Organizations may face challenges in collecting and analyzing the necessary data for informed decision-making.

- **Complexity:** In highly complex environments, the iterative and adaptive nature of empirical process control may introduce challenges in managing the intricacies of interconnected processes.

Summary

Empirical process control is a valuable approach in industries where change is constant, and uncertainty is a given. By embracing transparency, inspection, adaptation, and iteration, organizations can navigate the complexities of project management and process improvement with agility and responsiveness. As a foundational principle in agile methodologies and a mindset applicable across various domains, empirical process control empowers teams and organizations to learn from experience, continuously improve, and thrive in dynamic and unpredictable environments.

CHAPTER FOUR

Demystifying Cross-Functional Teams

Demystifying Cross-Functional Teams

In the ever-evolving landscape of modern business and project management, the concept of Cross-Functional Teams has emerged as a transformative approach to fostering collaboration, innovation, and efficiency. Unlike traditional teams organized around specific job functions or departments, cross-functional teams bring together individuals with diverse skills, backgrounds, and expertise to collectively tackle complex challenges. This chapter delves into the essence of cross-functional teams, exploring their definition, benefits, challenges, and best practices for optimal implementation.

Defining Cross-Functional Teams

A Cross-Functional Team is a group of individuals with diverse skills, roles, and functions, brought together to work on a common project or objective. Unlike traditional teams organized along departmental lines, cross-functional teams draw members from various disciplines, fostering collaboration and leveraging a spectrum of expertise to achieve a shared goal. Key characteristics, benefits, challenges and best practices of cross-functional teams are discussed in following sections.

Key Characteristics of Cross-Functional Teams:

- **Diversity of Skills:** Cross-functional teams comprise individuals with a range of skills and expertise relevant to the project's objectives. This diversity ensures a comprehensive approach to problem-solving and innovation.

- **Common Objective:** Members of cross-functional teams share a common goal or objective. This could be the successful delivery of a project, the development of a new product, or the resolution of a complex issue.

- **Collaboration Across Silos:** Cross-functional teams break down organizational silos by bringing together individuals from different departments or functional areas. This promotes seamless communication and collaboration.

- **Autonomy and Accountability:** Cross-functional teams are often granted a degree of autonomy in decision-making. Team members are collectively accountable for the outcomes of the project, fostering a sense of shared responsibility.

Benefits of Cross-Functional Teams:

- **Innovation and Creativity:** Diverse perspectives and skills within cross-functional teams stimulate innovation. The combination of varied experiences often leads to creative solutions and novel approaches to challenges.

- **Faster Decision-Making:** With individuals from different functional areas present, cross-functional teams can make decisions more rapidly. This agility is especially valuable in fast-paced environments.

- **Improved Problem-Solving:** Cross-functional teams excel at addressing complex problems. The variety of skills and viewpoints allows for a more comprehensive analysis of issues and the formulation of effective solutions.

- **Enhanced Flexibility:** Cross-functional teams are inherently flexible, adapting quickly to changes in project scope, requirements, or market conditions. This agility is a key asset in today's dynamic business landscape.

- **Knowledge Transfer:** Members of cross-functional teams have the opportunity to learn from each other. This knowledge transfer not only enhances individual skill sets but also strengthens the overall capabilities of the team.

- **Higher Employee Engagement:** Working in cross-functional teams can lead to increased job satisfaction and engagement. Team members often appreciate the opportunity to collaborate with colleagues outside their usual work sphere.

Challenges and Considerations:

- **Communication Barriers:** Diverse backgrounds can sometimes lead to communication challenges within cross-functional teams. Clear communication strategies, including regular updates and open channels, are crucial.

- **Conflict Resolution:** Differences in opinions and approaches may result in conflicts. Effective conflict resolution strategies, such as open dialogue and a collaborative problem-solving approach, are essential.

- **Resource Allocation:** Balancing resource allocation across different functions can be challenging. It's crucial to ensure that team members have the necessary resources and support to contribute effectively.

- **Establishing a Common Vision:** Aligning team members with different perspectives toward a common vision can be a complex task. Establishing a shared understanding of goals and objectives is essential for success.

Best Practices for Implementing Cross-Functional Teams:

- **Clear Definition of Roles:** Clearly define the roles and responsibilities of each team member to avoid ambiguity. This includes establishing leadership roles, if applicable, and ensuring everyone understands their contribution to the team.

- **Effective Leadership:** Leadership within cross-functional teams should focus on facilitation and empowerment. Leaders should foster a collaborative environment, encourage open communication, and ensure that the team stays aligned with its objectives.

- **Regular Communication:** Establish transparent and regular communication channels within the team. This includes scheduled meetings, updates, and opportunities for team members to share insights and challenges.

- **Shared Tools and Platforms:** Provide the team with shared tools and platforms to facilitate collaboration. This includes project management tools, communication platforms, and any other resources that support effective teamwork.

- **Inclusive Decision-Making:** Encourage inclusive decision-making processes that value input from all team members. Foster an environment where diverse perspectives are not only heard but actively sought out.

- **Continuous Learning and Improvement:** Promote a culture of continuous learning and improvement within the team. This includes regular retrospectives to reflect on what is working well and identify areas for enhancement.

Real-World Examples:

- **Product Development:** In product development, a cross-functional team may include individuals with expertise in design, engineering, marketing, and customer support. This ensures that all aspects of product creation and launch are considered.

- **Marketing Campaigns:** For a marketing campaign, a cross-functional team might bring together professionals from areas such as content creation, graphic design, social media management, and data analytics to create a comprehensive and effective strategy.

- **Software Development:** In software development, a cross-functional team could consist of developers, testers, user experience designers, and product owners. This structure ensures that the software meets both technical and user experience requirements.

The Modern Manager's Role in Cross-Functional Teams:

- **Facilitating Communication:** Effective communication is the cornerstone of successful cross-functional teams. Modern managers play a vital role in fostering an environment where open communication is encouraged, ensuring that information flows seamlessly between team members and functional areas.

- **Conflict Resolution:** The diversity inherent in cross-functional teams can sometimes lead to conflicts arising from differing perspectives. Managers must be adept at identifying and resolving conflicts promptly to maintain a positive team dynamic.

- **Encouraging Collaboration:** Modern managers must actively promote a culture of collaboration within cross-functional teams. This involves breaking down traditional hierarchies and encouraging team members to share knowledge, skills, and ideas freely.

- **Providing Strategic Direction:** While cross-functional teams are designed to be self-directed to a certain extent, managers still play a crucial role in providing overarching strategic direction. This involves aligning the team's efforts with the organization's overall objectives.

Differences from Traditional Teams and Management:

- **Hierarchy and Structure:** Traditional teams often operate within a rigid hierarchical structure, with clear lines of authority. Cross-functional teams, on the other hand, tend to have a flatter structure, promoting a more collaborative and egalitarian environment.

- **Focus on Specialization vs. Collaboration:** Traditional teams are often composed of members with similar skills and expertise. In contrast, cross-functional teams bring together individuals with diverse backgrounds, emphasizing collaboration and the integration of specialized knowledge.

- **Project-Centric vs. Departmental Silos:** Traditional teams are typically organized based on departmental functions, leading to a focus on individual tasks. Cross-functional teams are project-centric, concentrating on the successful completion of specific objectives rather than departmental silos.

Summary

As organizations continue to recognize the value of cross-functional teams in driving innovation and achieving strategic objectives, the role of the modern manager becomes increasingly pivotal. Managers must adapt their leadership styles to cultivate a culture of collaboration, open communication, and flexibility within these diverse teams. By doing so, they can harness the full potential of cross-functional teams and propel their organizations toward success in an ever-changing business landscape.

Demystifying Product Management

Product Management is a multifaceted discipline that plays a pivotal role in the development, delivery, and success of a product. In today's dynamic business environment, where innovation and customer satisfaction are paramount, the role of a Product Manager has become increasingly crucial. This chapter aims to provide a detailed exploration of Product Management, covering its definition, key responsibilities, and the skills required to excel in this field.

Defining Product Management:

Product Management can be defined as the strategic function within an organization responsible for guiding the development and evolution of a product throughout its lifecycle. It involves the intersection of business, technology, and user experience to ensure that a product not only meets the needs of its users but also aligns with the company's overall strategy and goals.

Key Responsibilities of a Product Manager:

- **Product Strategy and Vision:** Product Managers are responsible for defining the overall vision and strategy for a product. This includes understanding market trends, identifying opportunities, and setting clear goals for the product's success.

- **Market Research and Analysis:** Conducting thorough market research to identify customer needs, competitive landscape, and potential areas for innovation. This involves gathering and analyzing data to make informed decisions about the product's direction.

- **Roadmap and Planning:** Developing a product roadmap that outlines the planned features, enhancements, and releases over time. This involves prioritizing features based on business value and user impact.

- **Cross-Functional Collaboration:** Product Managers work closely with cross-functional teams, including engineering, design, marketing, and sales. Effective collaboration ensures that all teams are aligned and working toward the same product goals.

- **User Experience and Design:** Advocating for a positive user experience by collaborating with designers to create intuitive and user-friendly interfaces. Product Managers must ensure that the product not only meets functional requirements but also provides an excellent user experience.

- **Development Oversight:** Collaborating with development teams to ensure that the product is developed according to the specifications and meets quality standards. Product Managers often work with agile methodologies to facilitate iterative development.

- **Release Management:** Planning and coordinating product releases, including communication strategies, marketing campaigns, and user training. Product Managers ensure a smooth transition for users when new features are introduced.

- **Performance Monitoring and Optimization:** Continuously monitoring key performance indicators (KPIs) to assess the success of the product. Product Managers analyze user feedback and data to identify areas for improvement and optimization.

Essential Skills for Product Managers:

- **Strategic Thinking:** The ability to think strategically and align the product with the overall goals and vision of the company.

- **Communication and Collaboration:** Strong communication skills are essential for working with cross-functional teams, conveying the product vision, and gathering feedback from stakeholders.

- **Analytical Skills:** The capacity to analyze market data, user feedback, and performance metrics to make data-driven decisions.

- **Leadership:** Product Managers must lead without direct authority, inspiring and guiding cross-functional teams toward common goals.

- **User Empathy:** Understanding and empathizing with the needs and expectations of users to create a product that truly meets their requirements.

- **Adaptability:** The ability to adapt to changing market conditions, user feedback, and evolving business priorities.

Summary

Product Management is a dynamic and challenging field that requires a diverse skill set and a holistic approach to product development. Successful Product Managers are not only visionaries but also effective communicators, collaborators, and data-driven decision-makers. As companies strive for innovation and customer satisfaction, the role of Product Management continues to evolve, making it a central function in the success of modern businesses.

CHAPTER SIX

Value-Driven vs. Task-Driven

In the ever-evolving landscape of project management, two distinct approaches stand out: Value-Driven Delivery and Traditional Task-Driven methodologies. Each approach carries its own set of principles and perspectives, significantly impacting project outcomes. In this chapter, we delve into the key differences between these paradigms and explore why the shift toward value-driven delivery is gaining prominence in modern project management.

Understanding Traditional Task-Driven Approaches:

Traditionally, project management often centered around meticulous planning, defined tasks, and strict timelines. This task-driven approach involves breaking down projects into a sequence of individual tasks, assigning responsibilities, and tracking progress based on completion of these tasks. While this method provides a structured framework, it tends to focus more on activities than on the overall value delivered.

Key Characteristics of Traditional Task-Driven Approaches:

- **Sequential Planning:** Traditional methodologies emphasize comprehensive planning before execution, outlining a detailed roadmap of tasks.

- **Fixed Scope:** The project scope is typically defined upfront, and changes are often viewed as deviations from the plan.

- **Task Completion Metrics:** Progress is measured based on the completion of individual tasks and adherence to predefined schedules.

- **Limited Flexibility:** Adaptability to changing requirements or priorities is constrained due to the rigid nature of the predefined plan.

Embracing the Value-Driven Delivery Paradigm:

Value-Driven Delivery, on the other hand, shifts the focus from completing tasks to delivering tangible value to stakeholders. This approach places a premium on adaptability, collaboration, and continuous feedback, with the ultimate goal of maximizing value throughout the project lifecycle.

Key Characteristics of Value-Driven Delivery:

- **Iterative Planning:** Planning is done in short, iterative cycles, allowing for flexibility and adjustments based on evolving project needs.

- **Dynamic Scope:** The scope is considered flexible, and changes are embraced as a means of enhancing the overall value delivered.

- **Value Metrics:** Success is measured by the value generated for stakeholders, emphasizing outcomes over the completion of individual tasks.

- **Continuous Adaptation:** Value-Driven Delivery encourages constant adaptation to changing priorities, fostering a culture of continuous improvement.

Contrasts and Considerations:

- **Focus on Outcomes vs Activities:** Traditional approaches often emphasize completing tasks according to a predefined plan. In contrast, value-driven delivery prioritizes the outcomes achieved, valuing the impact of each task on the overall project goals.

- **Adaptability to Change:** Value-Driven Delivery is inherently more adaptable to change, with iterative planning allowing for adjustments based on feedback and evolving requirements. Traditional task-driven approaches may struggle to accommodate changes once the plan is set.

- **Stakeholder Collaboration:** Value-Driven Delivery places a strong emphasis on collaboration with stakeholders throughout the project. This collaborative approach ensures that the delivered product aligns closely with stakeholder expectations. Traditional task-driven methods might involve stakeholders primarily during the initial planning phase.

- **Risk Management:** Value-Driven Delivery inherently incorporates risk management through continuous adaptation and a focus on delivering incremental value. Traditional methodologies may rely on comprehensive upfront risk assessments, potentially missing emerging risks during execution.

Benefits of Embracing Value-Driven Delivery:

- **Increased Flexibility:** The iterative and adaptive nature of value-driven delivery allows for greater flexibility in responding to changing project dynamics.

- **Enhanced Stakeholder Satisfaction:** By prioritizing value delivery and incorporating stakeholder feedback throughout the project, the likelihood of meeting or exceeding stakeholder expectations is increased.

- **Continuous Improvement:** The emphasis on continuous adaptation and feedback loops in value-driven delivery promotes ongoing learning and improvement, contributing to better project outcomes over time.

- **Optimized Resource Utilization:** Value-driven delivery enables more efficient resource allocation by focusing efforts on high-priority tasks that contribute the most to overall project objectives.

Summary

As organizations strive for greater efficiency, adaptability, and stakeholder satisfaction, the shift from Traditional Task-Driven approaches to Value-Driven Delivery is becoming increasingly evident. While both approaches have their merits, the emphasis on delivering value over completing tasks positions value-driven delivery as a transformative force in the realm of modern project management. The key lies in understanding the unique requirements of each project and selecting the approach that aligns most effectively with the desired outcomes and stakeholder expectations.

CHAPTER SEVEN

Defined Process vs. Empirical Process

In the dynamic landscape of project management, Traditional Managers often find themselves grappling with various methodologies and frameworks. Two key approaches that demand attention are Defined Process and Empirical Process. Understanding the distinctions between these methodologies is crucial for managers aiming to optimize project outcomes. In this chapter, we delve into the core differences between Defined Process and Empirical Process to provide clarity for Traditional Managers.

Defined Process:

Defined Process is a structured and plan-driven approach to project management. In this methodology, the project team relies on a predefined set of processes and guidelines that are established before the project begins. The emphasis is on detailed planning, documentation, and adherence to a predetermined path. Traditional project management methods, such as the Waterfall model, are classic examples of Defined Process methodologies.

Key Characteristics of Defined Process:

- Predictability: The Defined Process is characterized by a high level of predictability. Project outcomes are anticipated and planned in advance, providing a clear roadmap for execution.

- Documentation: Rigorous documentation is a hallmark of Defined Process. Every aspect of the project is documented meticulously, aiding in accountability and knowledge transfer.

- Scope Stability: Defined Process works well when the project scope is stable and unlikely to change significantly throughout the project lifecycle.

Empirical Process:

Empirical Process, on the other hand, is an adaptive and iterative approach to project management. Unlike Defined Process, Empirical Process relies on continuous inspection and adaptation. This methodology is well-suited for projects where uncertainty is high, and requirements are likely to evolve. Agile methodologies, such as Scrum, exemplify the Empirical Process approach.

Key Characteristics of Empirical Process:

- **Adaptability:** Empirical Process thrives in environments where change is expected. It allows teams to adapt to evolving requirements and market conditions.

- **Continuous Feedback:** Regular inspection and adaptation are at the core of Empirical Process. Teams gather feedback regularly and adjust their approach based on the information received.

- **Customer Collaboration:** Empirical Process encourages collaboration with customers and stakeholders throughout the project, ensuring that the end product aligns closely with their evolving needs.

Choosing the Right Approach:

For Traditional Managers, the choice between Defined Process and Empirical Process depends on the nature of the project. Here are some factors to consider:

- **Project Stability:** If the project requirements are well-defined and unlikely to change, a Defined Process may be more appropriate. For projects with evolving requirements, Empirical Process is better suited.

- **Flexibility:** If adaptability is a priority and the project environment is dynamic, Empirical Process provides the necessary flexibility.

- **Customer Involvement:** If close collaboration with customers and stakeholders is crucial, as is often the case in industries like software development, Empirical Process is a preferred choice.

Summary

In the realm of project management, understanding the nuances between Defined Process and Empirical Process is essential for Traditional Managers. While Defined Process offers predictability and structure, Empirical Process thrives on adaptability and continuous improvement. The key is to choose the approach that aligns with the project's characteristics and goals, ensuring a successful and efficient management process from initiation to completion.

CHAPTER EIGHT

Classic Waterfall Project Management

Classic Waterfall Project Management

In the realm of project management methodologies, the Waterfall approach stands as one of the oldest and most structured methods for overseeing complex projects. Developed in the manufacturing and construction industries, Waterfall Project Management has since found application in diverse sectors, providing a systematic and linear framework for achieving project objectives. In this chapter, we will delve into the principles, characteristics, advantages, and challenges of Waterfall Project Management.

Origins and Development:

The Waterfall model traces its origins back to the 1950s and 1960s, a time when large-scale projects demanded a more systematic approach. Initially utilized in the fields of manufacturing and construction, the Waterfall methodology gained popularity as a sequential, step-by-step process for managing projects. Its name, "Waterfall," reflects the linear flow of tasks, where progress cascades downward, much like a waterfall.

Sequential Phases:

Waterfall Project Management is characterized by a sequential structure divided into distinct phases. These typically include:

- **Requirements:** Clearly defining and documenting project requirements.

- **Design:** Planning and designing the project based on specified requirements.

- **Implementation:** Executing the plans outlined in the design phase.

- **Verification:** Ensuring that the project meets the predefined requirements.

- **Maintenance:** Ongoing support, maintenance, and potential future enhancements.

Advantages of Waterfall Project Management:

- **Clarity and Structure:** The linear nature of Waterfall provides a clear roadmap for both project managers and team members.

- **Documentation:** Each phase necessitates comprehensive documentation, ensuring transparency and aiding future maintenance or upgrades.

- **Client Involvement:** Clients have a well-defined role at the beginning and end of the project, providing input during the requirements phase and reviewing the final product.

Challenges of Waterfall Project Management:

- **Limited Flexibility:** The rigid structure can be a drawback in dynamic environments where changes are frequent.

- **Late Adaptation to Feedback:** Limited opportunities for client feedback during development, potentially leading to misalignments with client expectations.

- **Extended Timelines:** The sequential nature may result in longer project timelines, especially if changes are requested late in the process.

Applicability in Today's Context:

While newer methodologies like Agile have gained popularity, Waterfall continues to find relevance in certain contexts. It is particularly suitable for projects where requirements are well-defined and changes are expected to be minimal. Industries such as construction, manufacturing, and critical infrastructure often benefit from the structured approach of Waterfall. In the ever-evolving landscape of project management methodologies, Waterfall Project Management holds its ground as a dependable and structured approach. Understanding its principles, advantages, and limitations is crucial for project managers seeking the most suitable methodology for their specific projects. While other agile methodologies offer more flexibility, the disciplined and systematic nature of Waterfall continues to make it a viable choice for projects with well-defined requirements and a linear progression towards success.

CHAPTER NINE

Downfall of Waterfall

Waterfall Project Management, a stalwart in the world of project management methodologies, has a rich history of successful implementation dating back to the mid-20th century. However, as the business landscape continues to evolve at an unprecedented pace, the rigid structure of Waterfall is being challenged by more agile and adaptive methodologies. In this chapter, we will explore the successes that propelled Waterfall to prominence and dissect the reasons behind its decreasing relevance in contemporary management practices.

Successes of Waterfall Project Management:

- a) **Clarity and Structure:** One of the key factors contributing to the success of Waterfall is its inherent clarity and structured approach. The sequential flow of phases, from requirements to maintenance, provided a roadmap that was easy to follow, ensuring that everyone involved had a clear understanding of project progression.

- b) **Comprehensive Documentation:** Waterfall's insistence on thorough documentation at each phase helped in maintaining a detailed record of the project. This not only facilitated effective communication within the team but also proved invaluable for future maintenance and troubleshooting.

- c) **Predictable Planning:** The step-by-step nature of Waterfall allowed for meticulous planning. Project managers could establish realistic timelines, allocate resources efficiently, and set clear expectations for stakeholders.

Why Waterfall is Becoming Outdated:

Limitations of Traditional Project Management

The business landscape is undergoing a profound transformation, marked by a shift towards agility and adaptability. While traditional project management methodologies have long been the bedrock of structured organizational processes, the rise of the Agile movement challenges the effectiveness of these conventional approaches. In this chapter, we explore the reasons why traditional project management may fall short in an Agile organization, where flexibility and responsiveness are paramount.

Rigidity in Planning:

- **Sequential Nature of Projects:** Traditional project management methods, often characterized by a linear progression of phases, may prove to be too rigid in an Agile environment. Agile principles emphasize adaptability and the ability to respond to change, which contrasts with the fixed nature of traditional project plans.

- **Fixed Scope and Requirements:** Traditional project management typically involves detailed upfront planning with fixed project scopes and requirements. In an Agile organization, where requirements are expected to evolve, this fixed approach can hinder the ability to respond quickly to shifting priorities or customer needs.

Limited Customer Collaboration:

- **Late Customer Feedback:** Traditional project management often involves minimal customer involvement until the later stages of the project. In contrast, Agile principles emphasize continuous customer collaboration throughout the development process, ensuring that the final product aligns closely with customer expectations.

- **Inflexible to Changing Customer Priorities:** Agile organizations prioritize responding to customer needs and changing market conditions. Traditional project management, with its predefined project plans, may struggle to accommodate shifting customer priorities without undergoing extensive re-planning.

Adapting to Change:

- **Change Management Challenges:** Traditional project management methodologies may struggle with changes in project scope, requirements, or priorities. Agile, on the other hand, is built on the premise that change is inevitable, and it provides a framework for incorporating changes seamlessly.

- **Risk of Project Failure:** In fast-paced industries where market dynamics change rapidly, the inability to adapt swiftly to unforeseen challenges can lead to project failure. Agile's iterative and incremental approach mitigates such risks by allowing for continuous reassessment and adaptation.

Team Collaboration and Empowerment:

- **Hierarchical Structures:** Traditional project management often adheres to hierarchical structures, with decision-making concentrated at the top. Agile principles promote self-organizing, cross-functional teams that collaborate closely, fostering a sense of empowerment and ownership among team members.

- **Lack of Flexibility in Team Roles:** In traditional project management, team roles are often predefined and specialized. Agile encourages flexibility in team roles, allowing members to take on different responsibilities based on the needs of the project.

Continuous Delivery vs. Fixed Milestones:

- **Fixed Milestones:** Traditional project management relies on fixed milestones and delivery dates. While this approach provides a clear timeline, it may not align with the iterative and incremental nature of Agile, which focuses on delivering value continuously throughout the project.

- **Iterative Development:** Agile organizations prioritize the early and continuous delivery of valuable features. This approach ensures that stakeholders receive tangible benefits at regular intervals rather than waiting for a project's completion.

In the era of rapid technological advancements and evolving customer expectations, the Agile approach has gained prominence for its ability to foster innovation, adaptability, and collaboration. While traditional project management methodologies have proven effective in certain contexts, they may fall short in meeting the demands of an Agile organization. Recognizing these limitations, organizations must carefully assess their projects, team structures, and customer engagement strategies to determine whether a shift towards Agile methodologies is essential for staying competitive and responsive in today's ever-changing business environment.

The Shift Towards Agile Methodologies:

- **Flexibility and Adaptability:** Agile methodologies, such as Scrum and Kanban, have gained traction due to their emphasis on flexibility and adaptability. Agile allows for iterative development, frequent client feedback, and the ability to pivot in response to changing requirements.

- **Collaborative Team Structures:** Agile encourages cross-functional collaboration, breaking down traditional silos and promoting a more collaborative environment. This contrasts with the more hierarchical and segmented approach of Waterfall.

- **Early Delivery of Value:** Agile's incremental approach enables the early delivery of functional components, providing tangible value to clients and stakeholders sooner in the development process.

• 37 •

Summary

While Waterfall Project Management played a crucial role in the development of project management methodologies, its inherent limitations have become more apparent in today's dynamic business environment. The shift towards more adaptive and collaborative approaches, such as Agile methodologies, reflects the need for organizations to stay nimble and responsive to change. As we bid farewell to the era of Waterfall dominance, the lessons learned from its successes and shortcomings will continue to shape the ever-evolving landscape of Project management.

CHAPTER TEN

The Iron Triangle Classic

The Iron Triangle, a classic concept in project management, represents the three key constraints of any project: scope, time, and cost. Traditionally, these constraints were seen as fixed and interdependent, forming a rigid framework that defined the success or failure of a project. However, with the rise of Agile methodologies, a paradigm shift has occurred, challenging the traditional notions of the Iron Triangle and allowing for greater flexibility and adaptability in project management.

The Traditional Iron Triangle:

- **Scope:** This refers to the defined features, functions, and deliverables of a project. Traditionally, the scope is determined at the beginning of a project and is expected to remain relatively fixed throughout its lifecycle.

- **Time:** The timeframe allocated for completing the project. Time constraints are often stringent, with deadlines and milestones set in advance to ensure timely delivery.

- **Cost:** The financial resources allocated to the project. Cost constraints are determined early in the project, and adhering to the budget is crucial for project success.

The Rigidity of the Traditional Model:

In the traditional project management model, the Iron Triangle implies a trade-off relationship among its three constraints. If one constraint changes, at least one other must adjust to maintain balance. For example, increasing the project scope might extend the timeline or require additional resources, thus affecting time and cost.

The Agile Approach:

Agile methodologies, such as Scrum and Kanban, introduce a dynamic shift in the way projects are managed. The Agile Manifesto, with its principles emphasizing individuals and interactions over processes and tools, values responding to change over following a plan. This shift challenges the fixed nature of the Iron Triangle.

- **Flexibility in Scope:** Agile acknowledges that requirements can change, and it embraces this change throughout the project. Instead of a fixed scope, Agile projects prioritize delivering the highest value features, allowing for adjustments based on evolving customer needs and market conditions.

- **Time-Boxed Iterations (Sprints):** Agile introduces the concept of time-boxed iterations, known as sprints. Each sprint has a fixed duration (typically two to four weeks), providing a regular cadence for delivering increments of value. This approach allows for adaptability in timelines while maintaining a steady rhythm of progress.

- **Iterative Cost Management:** Agile promotes adaptive financial planning. Rather than fixing the budget at the beginning, Agile projects continuously reassess priorities and allocate resources based on the evolving needs of the project.

The Agile Iron Triangle:

In the Agile paradigm, the Iron Triangle is often redefined with a new perspective:

- **Flexibility in Scope:** The Agile Iron Triangle recognizes that scope can change, and this flexibility is considered a positive attribute. The focus is on delivering the highest-priority features that align with customer needs and project goals.

- **Predictable Timeframes (Sprints):** While Agile embraces change, it does so within a structured framework. Sprints provide a predictable and regular cadence for delivering increments of value, allowing for adaptation while maintaining a sense of rhythm and predictability.

- **Adaptive Financial Planning:** Agile projects continuously reassess priorities and allocate resources based on changing requirements. This adaptive financial planning allows for a more dynamic response to project needs and reduces the risk of budget overruns.

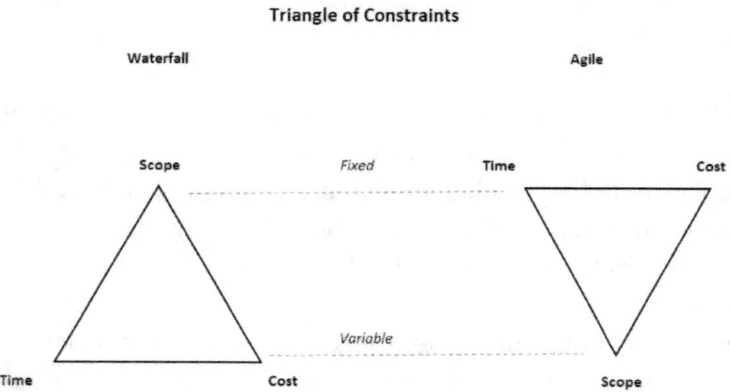

The Iron Triangle

Waterfall Iron Triangle vs Agile Iron Triangle

Summary

The Iron Triangle has long been a fundamental concept in project management, but the Agile paradigm challenges its fixed nature. Agile methodologies introduce a more flexible and adaptive approach to project management, enabling teams to respond to changing requirements, customer feedback, and market dynamics. By redefining the Iron Triangle with a focus on flexibility, predictability, and adaptive planning, Agile methodologies empower teams to navigate the complexities of project management in a rapidly changing world.

CHAPTER ELEVEN

Evolution of Agile Management

In the dynamic landscape of project management, Agile has emerged as a transformative force, revolutionizing how organizations approach complex projects. Born out of a need for flexibility, collaboration, and responsiveness, Agile Management has evolved over the years, reshaping traditional practices and fostering a culture of adaptability. This chapter explores the evolution of Agile Management, from its inception to its current status as a cornerstone in modern organizational methodologies.

Origins of Agile:

- **Manifesto for Agile Software Development:** The Agile Manifesto was officially launched in 2001, marking a pivotal moment in the field of software development. Conceived during a gathering of like-minded software practitioners at the Snowbird ski resort in Utah, the manifesto emerged as a response to the challenges and limitations of traditional, plan-driven methodologies. The manifesto encapsulated the group's shared values and principles, emphasizing a preference for individuals and interactions, working solutions, customer collaboration, and responsiveness to change over rigid processes and comprehensive documentation. This groundbreaking document laid the foundation for the Agile movement, promoting a more flexible and iterative approach to software development that prioritized adaptability, customer satisfaction, and continuous improvement. Since its launch, the Agile Manifesto has transcended its origins in software development and has been embraced across various industries as a guiding philosophy for fostering innovation and achieving project success.

- **Iterative and Incremental Development:** Agile methodologies, influenced by iterative and incremental development practices, focused on breaking down projects into smaller, manageable increments. This approach allowed for continuous reassessment and adaptation, fostering a more responsive and customer-centric development process.

Key Principles of Agile:

- **Adaptive Planning:** Agile embraces changing requirements, welcoming them even late in the development process. This flexibility enables teams to respond to evolving customer needs and market dynamics.

- **Collaborative Approach:** Agile emphasizes communication and collaboration among team members, clients, and stakeholders. Cross-functional teams work together to achieve common goals, breaking down silos that hinder progress.

- **Iterative Delivery:** The iterative nature of Agile allows for the incremental delivery of value. Products or features are delivered in small, functional pieces, ensuring that stakeholders receive tangible benefits early in the project lifecycle.

- **Continuous Improvement:** Agile encourages teams to regularly reflect on their processes and outcomes, fostering a culture of continuous improvement. Retrospectives and feedback loops enable teams to adapt and enhance their practices.

Agile Methodologies:

- **Scrum:** One of the most widely adopted Agile frameworks, Scrum introduces roles like Scrum Master and Product Owner, along with time-boxed iterations known as sprints. Scrum provides a structured yet flexible approach to product development.

- **Kanban:** Kanban, inspired by lean manufacturing principles, visualizes work on a board and focuses on limiting work in progress. It provides a more fluid approach to project management, allowing teams to pull work as capacity allows.

- **Extreme Programming (XP):** XP incorporates engineering practices such as pair programming and test-driven development. It emphasizes customer satisfaction, adaptability, and continuous feedback.

- **Agile Scaling:** Large-Scale Scrum (LeSS) and Scaled Agile Framework (SAFe): As organizations embraced Agile, the need for scaling Agile practices to large enterprises became apparent. Frameworks like LeSS and SAFe were developed to provide guidance on implementing Agile principles at scale.

Challenges and Criticisms:

- **Organizational Resistance:** The shift to Agile may face resistance from traditional organizational structures that are resistant to change.

- **Lack of Understanding:** Misinterpretation or inadequate understanding of Agile principles can lead to suboptimal implementations.

Future Trends:

- **Business Agility:** Organizations are increasingly adopting Agile not just for project management but as a holistic approach to business agility. This involves fostering a culture of adaptability, innovation, and collaboration throughout the organization.
- **DevOps Integration:** The integration of Agile with DevOps practices is becoming more prevalent, aiming for a seamless and continuous flow from development to deployment.

Summary

The evolution of Agile Management represents a paradigm shift in how organizations approach project management. Originally rooted in software development, Agile principles have transcended their initial domain and found applications in various business functions, including marketing, human resources, and finance. From its roots in software development to its widespread adoption across various industries, Agile has demonstrated its effectiveness in navigating the complexities of the modern business landscape. As organizations continue to strive for greater adaptability and customer satisfaction, Agile will undoubtedly remain at the forefront of innovative management methodologies, shaping the future of project management and organizational success.

CHAPTER TWELVE

The Agile Manifesto: History, Values, Principles

In the ever-evolving landscape of software development, the Agile Manifesto has emerged as a guiding philosophy that revolutionized how teams approach projects. Born out of a gathering of visionary minds in 2001, the Agile Manifesto represents a paradigm shift from traditional, plan-driven approaches to a more adaptive and collaborative methodology. In this chapter, we will delve into the history of the Agile Manifesto, its foundational values, and the twelve principles that have transformed the way teams approach software development.

A Brief History:

The Agile Manifesto originated from a group of software developers who sought a more effective way of working. In February 2001, seventeen individuals with diverse backgrounds and experiences gathered in Snowbird, Utah, to discuss lightweight development methods. The result of this gathering was the Agile Manifesto, a succinct declaration that emphasized individuals and interactions over processes and tools, working software over comprehensive documentation, customer collaboration over contract negotiation, and responding to change over following a plan.

The Four Core Values of the Agile Manifesto:

- **Individuals and Interactions over Processes and Tools:** The first value underscores the importance of prioritizing the people involved in the project and fostering effective communication and collaboration over relying solely on processes and tools.

- **Working Software over Comprehensive Documentation**: This value highlights the commitment to delivering tangible, functional software as the primary measure of progress, emphasizing the importance of practical results over exhaustive documentation.

- **Customer Collaboration over Contract Negotiation**: Agile places a premium on engaging customers throughout the development process. This value underscores the significance of collaboration with customers to ensure their evolving needs are met, rather than adhering strictly to predefined contracts.

- **Responding to Change over Following a Plan**: Agile recognizes the inevitability of change in the dynamic business environment. This value encourages teams to embrace change and adaptability, valuing the ability to respond to emerging requirements over rigidly adhering to a predetermined plan.

The Twelve Principles of the Agile Manifesto:

1. Our highest priority is to satisfy the customer through early and continuous delivery of valuable software.
2. Welcome changing requirements, even late in development. Agile processes harness change for the customer's competitive advantage.
3. Deliver working software frequently, from a couple of weeks to a couple of months, with a preference to the shorter timescale.
4. Business people and developers must work together daily throughout the project.
5. Build projects around motivated individuals. Give them the environment and support they need, and trust them to get the job done.
6. The most efficient and effective method of conveying information to and within a development team is face-to-face conversation.
7. Working software is the primary measure of progress.
8. Agile processes promote sustainable development. The sponsors, developers, and users should be able to maintain a constant pace

indefinitely.

9. Continuous attention to technical excellence and good design enhances agility.
10. Simplicity--the art of maximizing the amount of work not done--is essential.
11. The best architectures, requirements, and designs emerge from self-organizing teams.
12. At regular intervals, the team reflects on how to become more effective, then tunes and adjusts its behavior accordingly.

The Agile Manifesto, with its four core values and twelve principles, has left an indelible mark on the world of software development and beyond. It has inspired a cultural shift, encouraging teams to embrace collaboration, adaptability, and a relentless focus on delivering value. As organizations across various industries increasingly adopt agile methodologies, the principles of the Agile Manifesto continue to guide teams towards success in the ever-changing landscape of modern business.

Reference: https://agilemanifesto.org/

CHAPTER THIRTEEN

Agile Methodologies: Scrum Framework

In the realm of Agile methodologies, the Scrum framework stands out as a powerful and widely adopted approach to product development and management. Developed in the early 1990s by Jeff Sutherland and Ken Schwaber, Scrum has since revolutionized how teams approach complex projects. This chapter provides an in-depth examination of the history, key components, roles, and responsibilities within the Scrum framework.

History of Scrum:

The origins of Scrum can be traced back to a 1986 Harvard Business Review article by Hirotaka Takeuchi and Ikujiro Nonaka, who introduced the new flexible and holistic approach to product development. Jeff Sutherland and Ken Schwaber further refined and formalized these ideas into the Scrum framework in the early 1990s. Initially applied to software development, Scrum's success in delivering value quickly and responsively has led to its widespread adoption in various industries.

Key Components of the Scrum Framework:

Scrum Events:

- **Sprint:** The core time-boxed unit of work in Scrum is a Sprint, typically two to four weeks long. During a Sprint, a cross-functional team works on a set of prioritized items from the product backlog.

- **Sprint Planning:** At the beginning of each Sprint, the team conducts a Sprint Planning session to define the scope of work. This involves selecting backlog items and creating a Sprint Goal.

- **Daily Scrum:** A short daily stand-up meeting, the Daily Scrum, ensures team members synchronize their activities and discuss any impediments. It fosters communication and collaboration within the team.

- **Sprint Review:** At the end of each Sprint, a Sprint Review is held to demonstrate the completed work to stakeholders and gather feedback. This helps in adjusting priorities for the next Sprint.

- **Sprint Retrospective:** The Sprint Retrospective follows the Sprint Review and provides the team an opportunity to reflect on their processes and identify areas for improvement.

Scrum Roles:

- **Scrum Master:** The Scrum Master serves as a facilitator and coach for the Scrum team. Scrum Master remove impediments, foster collaboration, and ensure that the Scrum framework is adhered to.

- **Product Owner:** The Product Owner is responsible for defining and prioritizing the product backlog. Product Owner act as the voice of the customer, ensuring the team works on the most valuable features.

- **Development Team:** The Development Team consists of cross-functional members responsible for delivering the product increment. They self-organize and collaborate to achieve the Sprint Goal.

Responsibilities within the Scrum Framework

Product Owner Responsibilities:

- **Define Product Backlog:** The Product Owner creates and maintains a prioritized product backlog, representing the features, enhancements, and fixes needed for the product.

- **Stakeholder Communication:** They communicate with stakeholders to understand their needs and expectations, ensuring the product backlog reflects customer priorities.

- **Sprint Goal:** The Product Owner collaborates with the team to define a clear Sprint Goal for each iteration.

Scrum Master Responsibilities:

- **Facilitate Scrum Events:** The Scrum Master ensures that Scrum events are effectively conducted, guiding the team through Sprint Planning, Daily Scrum, Sprint Review, and Sprint Retrospective.

- **Remove Impediments:** Scrum Masters identify and eliminate obstacles that hinder the team's progress, creating a smooth working environment.

- **Promote Collaboration:** Fostering a culture of collaboration and continuous improvement is a key responsibility. Scrum Masters guide the team in adhering to Scrum principles.

Development Team Responsibilities:

- **Self-Organization:** Development Team members organize themselves to complete the work committed during the Sprint Planning.

- **Collaboration:** Team members collaborate across disciplines to deliver a potentially shippable product increment by the end of each Sprint.

- **Continuous Improvement:** The Development Team actively participates in Sprint Retrospectives to identify areas for improvement in their processes.

The Scrum framework has proven to be a game-changer in the world of Agile project management. Its iterative and incremental approach, combined with a focus on collaboration and responsiveness, has enabled teams to deliver high-quality products efficiently. By understanding the history, key components, and roles and responsibilities within the Scrum framework, organizations can harness its power to navigate the complexities of modern project development with agility and success. As Scrum continues to evolve, it remains a cornerstone methodology for those seeking to embrace adaptability and deliver value in an ever-changing business landscape.

What happens in the Scrum Events ?

Sprint Planning

Sprint Planning is a time-boxed event that occurs at the beginning of each sprint in the Scrum framework. Its primary objective is to define what the team will deliver during the sprint and how the work will be accomplished. The event is divided into two parts: Part 1 focuses on what can be delivered in the sprint, and Part 2 is dedicated to how the chosen work will be achieved.

Roles and Responsibilities

Scrum Master: Facilitator and Servant Leader

- **Facilitator:** The Scrum Master plays a crucial role in ensuring the Sprint Planning event runs smoothly. They facilitate the discussions, guide the team through the process, and ensure that everyone is aligned with the goals of the sprint.

- **Servant Leader:** The Scrum Master acts as a servant leader, helping the team by removing impediments and promoting a collaborative environment. They ensure that the team is self-organizing and empowered to make decisions.

Product Owner: Visionary and Decision-maker

- **Visionary:** The Product Owner brings the product vision to the Sprint Planning meeting. They articulate the product backlog items and prioritize them based on the overall goals and objectives of the project.

- **Decision-maker:** During Sprint Planning, the Product Owner helps the team understand the priorities and makes decisions on what features or user stories will be included in the upcoming sprint. They provide the necessary context for the team to make informed choices.

Development Team: Collaborators and Executors

- **Collaborators:** The development team actively participates in Sprint Planning, engaging in discussions with the Product Owner to gain a clear understanding of the requirements and priorities. They share their insights on what can be achieved within the sprint based on their capacity and past performance.

- **Executors:** Once the scope is agreed upon, the development team takes ownership of the committed work. They break down the selected product backlog items into tasks, estimate effort, and create a plan for the sprint.

Sprint Planning Activities

Part 1: What can be delivered?

- **Review of the Product Backlog:** The Product Owner presents the highest-priority items in the product backlog to the team. The team seeks clarification on any uncertainties or ambiguities in the requirements.

- **Capacity Planning:** The development team assesses its capacity for the sprint based on past performance, taking into account factors like team velocity, individual availability, and any potential disruptions.

- **Definition of Done (DoD):** The team ensures a shared understanding of the Definition of Done for the selected product backlog items, setting the quality standards for the sprint.

Part 2: How will the work be achieved?

Task Decomposition: The development team collaboratively breaks down the selected product backlog items into smaller, manageable tasks. This detailed breakdown facilitates a more accurate estimation of effort and provides clarity on the work required.

Estimation: The team estimates the effort required for each task using techniques like story points or time-based estimates. This helps in planning the workload and setting expectations for the sprint.

Commitment: The team, along with the Product Owner, makes a commitment to the scope of work for the sprint. This commitment is based on a realistic assessment of what can be achieved within the given time frame.

Sprint Planning is a pivotal event in the Scrum framework, laying the foundation for a successful sprint. Through effective collaboration and communication, the Scrum Master, Product Owner, and development team work together to define a clear plan and commitment for the upcoming iteration. The structured approach of Sprint Planning fosters transparency, accountability, and adaptability, allowing development teams to respond efficiently to changing requirements and deliver high-quality products.

***

Sprint Review

The Sprint Review is a time-boxed event held at the end of each sprint in the Scrum framework. Unlike other ceremonies, the Sprint Review is an opportunity for the Scrum Team to present the completed work to stakeholders, gather feedback, and collaboratively plan the next steps. It serves as a bridge between the development team and the stakeholders, fostering transparency and ensuring that the delivered increments align with the product's vision.

Roles and Responsibilities

Scrum Master: Facilitator and Servant Leader

- **Facilitator:** The Scrum Master plays a pivotal role in facilitating the Sprint Review event. They ensure that the session is well-organized, focused, and conducive to collaboration. The Scrum Master may also help manage time effectively to cover all necessary aspects of the review.

- **Servant Leader:** As a servant leader, the Scrum Master supports the development team and stakeholders during the Sprint Review. They aim to remove any impediments that may hinder effective communication and collaboration, promoting an environment where feedback can be openly shared.

Product Owner: Stakeholder Liaison and Vision Keeper

- **Stakeholder Liaison:** The Product Owner actively participates in the Sprint Review to provide context and answer questions from stakeholders. They serve as a bridge between the development team and the broader business context, helping stakeholders understand the value delivered in the increment.

- **Vision Keeper:** The Product Owner ensures that the completed work aligns with the overall vision and goals of the product. They may discuss the product backlog, potential changes in priorities, and provide insights into the roadmap for future sprints.

Development Team: Demonstrators and Collaborators

- **Demonstrators:** The development team takes center stage during the Sprint Review, presenting the completed work to stakeholders. They showcase the increment, highlighting new features, improvements, or changes that have been implemented during the sprint.

- **Collaborators:** The development team actively engages with stakeholders, gathering feedback, answering questions, and incorporating suggestions for improvement. This collaboration helps build a shared understanding between the team and stakeholders, fostering a sense of collective ownership.

Sprint Review Activities

- **Product Increment Demonstration:** The development team demonstrates the product increment that has been completed during the sprint. This demonstration showcases the tangible results of the team's efforts, allowing stakeholders to see the product in action.

- **Feedback and Discussion:** Stakeholders provide feedback on the demonstrated increment. This feedback can be related to functionality, design, or any other aspect of the product. The development team and Product Owner actively listen, respond to queries, and take note of valuable insights.

- **Review of Product Backlog:** The Product Owner may discuss the product backlog, providing insights into potential changes in priorities or upcoming features. This discussion helps stakeholders understand the broader context and the future direction of the product.

The Sprint Review event in the Scrum framework serves as a dynamic forum for collaboration, transparency, and continuous improvement. By actively involving stakeholders in the review process, the Scrum Team ensures that the delivered increment aligns with expectations and adds value to the product. The Sprint Review is not just a ceremony to mark the end of a sprint; it is a strategic opportunity for the Scrum Team to engage with stakeholders, gather insights, and refine their approach for the next iteration, embodying the principles of agility and responsiveness.

***

Sprint Retrospective

The Sprint Retrospective is a time-boxed event that occurs at the end of each sprint in the Scrum framework. Its primary goal is to enable the team to inspect and adapt by reflecting on the experiences of the just-completed sprint. The focus is on identifying what went well, what could be improved, and determining concrete actions to enhance the team's effectiveness and collaboration in the upcoming sprints.

Roles and Responsibilities

Scrum Master: Facilitator and Catalyst for Improvement

- **Facilitator:** The Scrum Master takes on the role of a facilitator during the Sprint Retrospective. They guide the team through the retrospective process, ensuring that the discussion remains focused, constructive, and respectful.

- **Catalyst for Improvement:** The Scrum Master helps the team identify areas for improvement and encourages open and honest communication. They play a pivotal role in fostering a culture of continuous improvement within the Scrum Team.

Development Team: Active Participants and Stakeholders

- **Active Participants:** All members of the development team actively participate in the retrospective, sharing their insights and perspectives on the sprint. This inclusivity is vital for a comprehensive understanding of the team's dynamics and performance.

- **Stakeholders:** The development team is not only responsible for sharing their individual experiences but also for actively engaging in discussions around team dynamics, collaboration, and processes that impact the overall sprint outcome.

Sprint Retrospective Activities

- **Review of the Sprint:** The Scrum Team begins by reviewing the just-completed sprint. This includes a discussion of the achieved goals, the product increment delivered, and any challenges or impediments encountered during the sprint.

- **Identification of What Went Well:** Team members collectively identify and discuss aspects of the sprint that went well. This could include successful collaborations, efficient problem-solving, or the completion of tasks ahead of schedule. Acknowledging these positive aspects helps the scrum team to reinforce successful practices.

- **Identification of Areas for Improvement:** The team then turns its focus to areas that could be improved. This may involve discussing challenges, bottlenecks, or breakdowns in communication. The goal is to identify specific issues that, if addressed, could enhance the team's overall performance.

- **Action Planning:** Based on the insights gained from the retrospective, the Scrum Team collaboratively creates a list of actionable items for improvement. These action items should be specific, measurable, achievable, relevant, and time-bound (SMART). Each team member may commit to taking ownership of one or more action items.

- **Closure and Appreciation:** The retrospective concludes with a sense of closure and appreciation. Team members express gratitude for each other's efforts and contributions during the sprint. This positive closure fosters a sense of camaraderie and reinforces a culture of mutual respect and appreciation.

The Sprint Retrospective in the Scrum framework is more than just a retrospective review; it is a catalyst for continuous improvement. By providing a structured and collaborative space for reflection, the Scrum Team can evolve and adapt to changing circumstances, ensuring that each sprint brings not only incremental product improvements but also enhanced teamwork and efficiency. The Sprint Retrospective, when approached with sincerity and a commitment to improvement, becomes a cornerstone for building a resilient and high-performing Scrum Team.

***

Daily Scrum

The Daily Scrum, also known as the Daily Standup, is a brief and focused event that occurs every day during a sprint in the Scrum framework. Its primary objective is to provide a forum for the development team to align their efforts, inspect progress, and adapt their plans as needed. This daily rhythm promotes communication, collaboration, and transparency, fostering a shared understanding of the sprint goals and individual contributions.

Roles and Responsibilities

Development Team: Collaborators and Coordinators

- **Collaborators:** All members of the development team actively participate in the Daily Scrum. Each team member shares updates on their progress since the last meeting, focusing on what they did yesterday, what they plan to do today, and any impediments they are facing.

- **Coordinators:** The development team uses the Daily Scrum as a coordination point, ensuring that everyone is aware of what their teammates are working on. This facilitates collaboration, prevents duplication of efforts, and helps identify dependencies.

Scrum Master: Facilitator and Impediment Remover

- **Facilitator:** The Scrum Master takes on the role of a facilitator during the Daily Scrum. They ensure that the meeting stays within the time-box (usually 15 minutes or less) and that team members focus on the key aspects of progress, plans, and impediments.

- **Impediment Remover:** If any team member highlights impediments during the Daily Scrum, the Scrum Master notes these challenges and works to remove them promptly. This proactive approach is essential for keeping the team's progress unhindered.

Product Owner: Observer and Contributor

- **Observer:** While the Product Owner is not required to actively participate in the Daily Scrum, they may attend as an observer. This allows them to stay informed about the team's progress and any challenges they may be facing.

- **Contributor:** If team members have questions or need clarification on user stories or acceptance criteria, the Product Owner can use the Daily Scrum as an opportunity to provide additional information. Their insights contribute to a clearer understanding of the sprint goals.

Since this Daily Scrum is the shortest event of 15 minutes or less the Teams can follow their customized approach for this event which helps them to complete the event quickly.

***

CHAPTER FOURTEEN

Agile Methodologies: Kanban

Agile Methodologies: Kanban

In the realm of Agile methodologies, Kanban has emerged as a powerful and adaptable approach to managing work processes. Originating from lean manufacturing principles, Kanban has undergone significant evolution to become a cornerstone of Agile management. This chapter delves into the history, key principles, and evolution of the Kanban process in Agile management.

The Historical Roots of Kanban:

The term "Kanban" traces its roots to the Japanese manufacturing industry, particularly the Toyota Production System (TPS). In the 1940s, Toyota engineer Taiichi Ohno developed a system to improve manufacturing efficiency. The word "Kanban" itself translates to "visual card" or "signboard" in Japanese, representing the visual cues used to signal the need for production in a just-in-time system.

Evolution of Kanban in Manufacturing:

Visualizing Workflow:

- Card-Based System: The earliest Kanban systems utilized physical cards to represent work items and their progress through the production process. These cards acted as signals for replenishing materials or triggering the next production step.

- Pull System: Kanban introduced the concept of a "pull" system, where production is initiated based on actual demand rather than forecasting. This minimized waste and overproduction, core tenets of lean manufacturing.

Kanban's Transition to Agile Management:

Software Development Adoption: David J. Anderson's Contribution: In the early 2000s, David J. Anderson adapted Kanban principles to software development. He introduced the Kanban Method, which emphasized visualizing workflow, limiting work in progress (WIP), and using metrics to improve efficiency.

Core Principles of Kanban in Agile:

- Visual Board: Kanban retains its core principle of visualizing work on a board. In Agile management, this translates into a visual representation of tasks on a board, typically divided into columns representing different stages of the workflow.

- Work in Progress (WIP) Limits: Kanban advocates setting limits on the number of tasks allowed in each workflow stage simultaneously. This prevents overloading and fosters a focus on completing existing work before taking on new tasks.

- Continuous Flow: The emphasis on a continuous and smooth flow of work items remains a key Kanban principle. This contrasts with iterative development cycles seen in other Agile frameworks like Scrum.

Kanban vs. Scrum:

- Flexibility: Kanban offers greater flexibility compared to Scrum. While Scrum operates in fixed time-boxed iterations (sprints), Kanban allows for a continuous flow of work.

- Roles and Ceremonies: Scrum defines specific roles and ceremonies, such as Scrum Master and Sprint Planning. Kanban, on the other hand, provides a more adaptive framework without prescribing specific roles or ceremonies.

- Iterative vs. Continuous Improvement: Scrum emphasizes iterative improvement through retrospectives at the end of each sprint. In Kanban, improvement is continuous, with teams encouraged to make incremental changes as needed.

Current Trends and Future Directions:

Widespread Adoption:

- Beyond Software Development: Kanban has expanded beyond software development to various industries, including marketing, human resources, and customer support, emphasizing its versatility.

- Enterprise-Level Adoption: Large organizations have embraced Kanban for managing complex workflows at the enterprise level, contributing to its ongoing evolution.

Integration with Agile and DevOps:

- **Agile & Kanban Synergy:** Organizations often integrate Kanban with other Agile methodologies, creating a hybrid approach that combines the flexibility of Kanban with the structured planning of Agile.

- **DevOps Alignment:** Kanban's emphasis on continuous flow aligns seamlessly with DevOps practices, promoting a smooth transition from development to deployment.

The journey of Kanban from its roots in Japanese manufacturing to its prominent place in Agile management is a testament to its adaptability and effectiveness. As organizations seek more flexible and responsive ways to manage work processes, Kanban continues to evolve, demonstrating its enduring relevance in an ever-changing business landscape. Whether applied to software development or enterprise-level workflows, Kanban's principles of visualizing work, limiting WIP, and ensuring a continuous flow have become integral to fostering efficiency and adaptability in the world of Agile management.

CHAPTER FIFTEEN

Agile Methodologies: Lean Development

In the pursuit of efficiency, waste reduction, and continuous improvement, the Lean philosophy has played a pivotal role in reshaping management approaches across various industries. Originating from manufacturing, Lean processes have evolved over time and found a natural integration into the Agile management framework. This chapter explores the rich history, key principles, and the evolution of Lean processes in the context of Agile management.

Historical Roots of Lean Processes

Toyota Production System (TPS):

- Post-WWII Japan: The origins of Lean can be traced back to post-World War II Japan when Toyota faced resource constraints and a need for efficient production.

- Taiichi Ohno's Contributions: Engineer Taiichi Ohno, along with Shigeo Shingo, developed the Toyota Production System (TPS), laying the foundation for Lean manufacturing.

Key Principles of Lean:

- **Waste Reduction (Muda):** Lean focuses on minimizing waste, be it in the form of overproduction, unnecessary inventory, defects, or excess processing.

- **Just-in-Time (JIT):** The JIT principle involves producing items exactly when they are needed, eliminating the need for excess inventory and reducing carrying costs.

- **Continuous Improvement (Kaizen):** Kaizen encourages a culture of continuous improvement, where small, incremental changes are made consistently to enhance efficiency and quality.

Evolution of Lean Processes in Agile Management

Lean in Software Development:

- **Mary and Tom Poppendieck:** In the early 2000s, Mary and Tom Poppendieck applied Lean principles to software development, emphasizing the need for flexibility, customer focus, and value delivery.

- **Reduction of Waste in Code:** Lean principles translated into the software development context by addressing waste in code through practices like minimizing defects, improving collaboration, and enhancing code simplicity.

Lean and Agile Synergy:

- **Agile Manifesto:** The Agile Manifesto, created in 2001 by a group of software developers, emphasized values such as individuals and interactions, working solutions, and customer collaboration over processes and tools.

- **Common Goals:** Lean and Agile share common goals, including the prioritization of customer value, responsiveness to change, and a focus on delivering high-quality products.

- **Kanban in Agile:** The integration of Kanban, a Lean-inspired visual management tool, into Agile methodologies exemplifies the synergy between Lean and Agile principles.

Lean-Agile Frameworks:

- **SAFe (Scaled Agile Framework):** SAFe, a popular Agile scaling framework, incorporates Lean principles by emphasizing value delivery, systems thinking, and lean-agile leadership.

- **Lean Portfolio Management:** Lean Portfolio Management (LPM) extends Lean principles to the strategic level, aligning business strategy with the execution of value streams.

Lean Thinking Beyond IT:

- **Lean Startups:** Beyond software development, Lean principles have influenced startup culture, encouraging a focus on customer feedback, minimal viable products, and rapid iterations.

- **Lean in Healthcare, Manufacturing, and Beyond:** Lean has transcended its origins in software development, finding applications in various industries, including healthcare, manufacturing, and services.

Continuous Evolution:

- **Lean-Agile Mindset:** Organizations adopting a Lean-Agile mindset continuously evolve, emphasizing adaptability, collaboration, and a commitment to delivering value.

- **Emergence of Lean-Agile Leadership:** Lean-Agile leadership emphasizes servant leadership, where leaders enable and empower teams to achieve their best through Lean and Agile principles.

The history and evolution of Lean processes in Agile management reflect a journey of continuous improvement and adaptability. From its origins in post-war Japan to its integration into modern software development and beyond, Lean principles have left an indelible mark on how organizations approach efficiency and value delivery. As Lean continues to evolve within the Agile landscape, its core tenets of waste reduction, just-in-time delivery, and continuous improvement remain pivotal in fostering a culture of agility and excellence. In a world that demands responsiveness and innovation, Lean processes continue to provide a roadmap for organizations seeking to thrive in the ever-changing landscape of Agile management.

CHAPTER SIXTEEN

Agile Methodologies: Extreme Programming

Agile Methodologies: Extreme Programming

In the dynamic landscape of Agile methodologies, Extreme Programming (XP) stands out as a bold and innovative approach to software development. Developed in the late 1990s by Kent Beck, XP has significantly influenced the Agile movement, redefining how teams approach software development. This chapter takes a deep dive into the history, key principles, and the evolution of Extreme Programming within the context of Agile management.

The Genesis of Extreme Programming:

Kent Beck and the XP Principles:

- **Smalltalk Programming:** Kent Beck, an American software engineer, began developing Extreme Programming principles while working with Smalltalk programming language.
- **XP as a Response to Challenges:** Beck's motivation for XP was to address common challenges in software development, such as changing requirements, slow feedback loops, and a lack of adaptability.

Key Principles of Extreme Programming:

- **Simplicity:** XP emphasizes the principle of Keep It Simple, promoting the simplest solutions that fulfill the requirements.

- **Feedback Loops:** Rapid and continuous feedback is a core tenet of XP. This involves regular communication with customers, testing, and constant integration to identify and address issues promptly.

- **Continuous Planning:** Rather than extensive upfront planning, XP embraces continuous planning, where plans evolve as the project progresses and as new information becomes available.

- **Pair Programming:** In XP, developers work in pairs, with one writing the code and the other reviewing it in real-time. This practice enhances code quality, encourages knowledge sharing, and reduces defects.
- **Test-Driven Development (TDD):** TDD involves writing tests before writing the code. This practice ensures that code meets the specified requirements and facilitates easier maintenance.

Evolution of Extreme Programming in Agile Management:

Integration with Agile Manifesto:

- **Agile Manifesto:** Extreme Programming aligns closely with the values and principles outlined in the Agile Manifesto, emphasizing customer collaboration, responding to change, and delivering working software.

- **Agile Principles in XP:** XP embodies several Agile principles, such as delivering working software frequently, maintaining a sustainable pace of work, and prioritizing individuals and interactions.

Challenges and Adaptations:

- **Broader Applicability:** While initially associated with small, co-located teams, XP principles have been adapted to suit a broader range of project types, including distributed and large-scale development efforts.

- **Integration with Other Agile Frameworks:** XP is often integrated with other Agile frameworks, such as Scrum and Kanban, to tailor practices to specific project requirements.

Influence on Agile Practices:

- **Continuous Integration:** The XP practice of continuous integration, where code changes are frequently integrated into a shared repository, has become a standard practice in Agile software development.

- **Iterative Development:** XP's iterative approach, with frequent releases and updates, has influenced Agile methodologies, emphasizing incremental development and delivering value in short iterations.

Agile Development at Scale:

- **Large-Scale XP (LeSS):** Large-Scale XP, or LeSS, extends XP principles to address the challenges of scaling Agile practices to larger organizations and complex projects.

- **SAFe Integration:** XP practices have found a place in Scaled Agile Framework (SAFe), contributing to its emphasis on lean-agile development.

Modern Application Beyond Software Development:

- **XP in Non-Software Domains:** XP practices have been applied beyond software development, influencing domains such as product management, marketing, and organizational leadership.

- **Lean Thinking Integration:** The Lean thinking embedded in XP has gained traction beyond software, inspiring a lean-agile mindset in various industries.

Extreme Programming's journey from its inception in the late 1990s to its integration into the broader Agile landscape is a testament to its enduring principles of simplicity, rapid feedback, and continuous improvement. As organizations seek efficient and adaptive approaches to software development, XP's influence on Agile practices continues to resonate. In an era of ever-evolving technology and changing customer needs, the principles of Extreme Programming remain relevant, offering a roadmap for teams and organizations committed to delivering high-quality software in an agile and responsive manner.

CHAPTER SEVENTEEN

Project Managers Embracing New Opportunities

In the ever-evolving landscape of management, traditional managers find themselves at a crossroads where embracing new roles is not just a choice but a necessity. The dynamics of the business world, characterized by rapid technological advancements, changing consumer demands, and a focus on agility, have given rise to a plethora of management opportunities beyond the traditional scope. This chapter explores the exciting avenues available for traditional managers, ranging from Agile Practitioner and Product Owner to Scrum Master, Servant Leader, Change Management Professional, and Program Manager.

Agile Practitioner:

The Agile approach has become synonymous with adaptability and responsiveness. Traditional managers can transition into Agile Practitioners by mastering Agile methodologies such as Scrum or Kanban. This role involves facilitating collaboration, fostering a culture of continuous improvement, and ensuring the team is equipped to deliver value in a fast-paced environment.

Product Owner:

Stepping into the shoes of a Product Owner involves a shift towards a more strategic and customer-focused mindset. Product Owners are responsible for defining and prioritizing features, ensuring alignment with business goals, and maximizing the value delivered by the product. Traditional managers can leverage their functional expertise to excel in this pivotal role.

Scrum Master:

The Scrum Master role is integral to the successful implementation of Scrum methodology. It goes beyond traditional management by focusing on removing impediments, facilitating team interactions, and promoting a culture of continuous improvement. Transitioning to a Scrum Master role allows managers to guide teams in their journey towards greater efficiency and innovation.

Servant Leader:

Embracing the philosophy of servant leadership entails putting the needs of the team first. Traditional managers can evolve into Servant Leaders by prioritizing the growth and development of their team members, fostering a collaborative environment, and empowering individuals to contribute their best work. This approach aligns with the principles of Agile and promotes a culture of shared success.

Change Management Professional:

The ability to navigate and guide teams through change is a valuable skill in the modern business landscape. Transitioning to a Change Management Professional involves understanding the human side of change, designing effective communication strategies, and creating plans to mitigate resistance. Traditional managers can play a pivotal role in ensuring successful organizational transitions.

Program Manager:

As organizations undertake multiple projects to achieve strategic goals, the role of a Program Manager becomes increasingly vital. Traditional managers can leverage their experience in overseeing projects to transition into Program Managers, responsible for coordinating and aligning various projects to deliver cohesive outcomes that contribute to overarching business objectives.

Summary

In a summary, the transformation of traditional managers into Agile Practitioners, Product Owners, Scrum Masters, Servant Leaders, Change Management Professionals, and Program Managers is indicative of a broader shift in management paradigms. Embracing these roles offers managers the opportunity to thrive in dynamic environments, foster innovation, and contribute to organizational success. The adaptability and diverse skill set of traditional managers position them as valuable assets in the modern business landscape, where the ability to lead, inspire, and drive change is more crucial than ever. As the saying goes, "The only constant in life is change," and for traditional managers, the path to success lies in their ability to evolve and embrace the multitude of opportunities that the changing management landscape presents. More detailed information is provided on the various roles of Agile Management in next chapters.

CHAPTER EIGHTEEN

Product Backlog & Backlog Refinement

In the realm of agile product development, the Product Backlog serves as a central element, guiding the evolution of a product from conception to delivery. This dynamic and prioritized list of features, enhancements, and user stories provides a roadmap for development teams. To ensure the effectiveness of the Product Backlog, the practice of Backlog Refinement plays a pivotal role. This chapter delves into the concepts of the Product Backlog and Backlog Refinement, exploring their significance, best practices, and their impact on the success of agile projects.

The Product Backlog: Blueprint for Agile Success

The Product Backlog is a prioritized list of all the features, enhancements, bug fixes, and technical tasks that need to be addressed in a product. It serves as the single source of truth for the development team, product owner, and stakeholders regarding the work that needs to be completed. The items in the Product Backlog are often represented as user stories, each capturing a piece of functionality from an end-user's perspective.

Characteristics of a Well-Managed Product Backlog

- **Prioritization:** Items in the Product Backlog are ordered based on their importance and value to the product and its users. High-priority items are placed at the top, ensuring the team focuses on the most valuable work first.

- **Dynamic Nature:** The Product Backlog is not static; it evolves as the product and project progress. New items are added, and existing ones are refined or reprioritized based on changing requirements, feedback, and market conditions.
- **Granularity:** Each item in the Product Backlog should be sufficiently granular to represent a deliverable piece of functionality. This granularity enables the team to estimate effort accurately and facilitates effective sprint planning.
- **Collaborative Ownership:** While the Product Owner is responsible for maintaining the Product Backlog, it is a collaborative effort. Regular engagement with stakeholders, development teams, and scrum masters ensures alignment with overall project goals.

Backlog Refinement: Sculpting the Path to Success

- Backlog Refinement, also known as Backlog Grooming, is an ongoing process where the Product Backlog is reviewed, updated, and refined to ensure its readiness for upcoming sprints. This practice allows the team to clarify requirements, remove ambiguity, and make necessary adjustments to keep the backlog in optimal condition.

Activities Involved in Backlog Refinement

- **Addition of New Items:** Stakeholders may introduce new ideas, features, or requirements that need to be captured in the Product Backlog. Backlog Refinement sessions provide a platform to discuss and incorporate these new items.

- **Detailed Estimation:** Development teams use Backlog Refinement sessions to provide detailed estimates for the effort required to complete each backlog item. This aids in prioritization and sprint planning.

- **Clarification of Requirements:** Ambiguous or unclear backlog items are refined to ensure that everyone in the team has a shared understanding of the requirements. This reduces the likelihood of misunderstandings during development.

- **Prioritization Adjustments:** Based on changing business priorities or emerging market trends, the Product Owner may need to adjust the prioritization of backlog items. Backlog Refinement sessions facilitate discussions on these adjustments.

- **Splitting and Consolidating Items:** Large or complex backlog items may need to be split into smaller, more manageable pieces. Conversely, multiple smaller items may be consolidated to streamline development and improve clarity.

- **Dependency Identification:** Backlog Refinement helps identify dependencies between backlog items. Understanding these dependencies is crucial for effective sprint planning and ensures that teams can deliver valuable increments of work.

Best Practices for Backlog Refinement

- **Regular Sessions:** Conduct Backlog Refinement sessions regularly, ideally once per sprint or as needed. This ensures that the Product Backlog remains up-to-date and ready for upcoming sprints.
- **Inclusive Participation:** Encourage the active participation of the entire team, including developers, testers, and other relevant stakeholders, in Backlog Refinement sessions. Diverse perspectives contribute to better refinement.
- **Timeboxing:** Set a time limit for each Backlog Refinement session to avoid excessive discussions and ensure that the team remains focused on the most critical items.
- **Continuous Communication:** Foster open communication between team members and stakeholders throughout the refinement process. Addressing questions and concerns promptly helps maintain a healthy and collaborative environment.
- **The Symbiotic Relationship:** The Product Backlog and Backlog Refinement share a symbiotic relationship, each influencing the

effectiveness of the other. A well-managed Product Backlog serves as a reliable guide for the team, ensuring that they are working on the most valuable items. Backlog Refinement, in turn, keeps the Product Backlog in a state of constant readiness, facilitating smooth sprint planning and execution.

Summary

In the dynamic world of agile development, the Product Backlog and Backlog Refinement emerge as critical tools for success. By fostering collaboration, adaptability, and continuous improvement, these practices empower teams to navigate complexity and deliver products that truly meet the needs of users and stakeholders. As organizations continue to embrace agile methodologies, the mastery of Product Backlog management and Backlog Refinement becomes an indispensable skill.

Understanding User Story Points & Velocity

In the dynamic world of Scrum, an Agile framework for managing complex projects, two key concepts play a pivotal role in planning and execution: User Story Points and Sprint Velocity. These concepts are integral to estimating, planning, and tracking progress in Scrum, providing teams with valuable insights into their capacity and performance. This chapter delves into the intricacies of User Story Points and Sprint Velocity, exploring their definitions, significance, and how they contribute to the success of Scrum teams.

User Story Points

User Story Points are a unit of measure used by Scrum teams to estimate the relative effort required to implement a user story. Unlike traditional time-based estimates, such as hours or days, User Story Points represent the complexity, effort, and uncertainty associated with a particular piece of work. This approach allows teams to focus on the relative size and difficulty of tasks rather than getting bogged down by precise time estimations.

Key Characteristics of Story Points

- **Relative Sizing:** User Story Points are assigned based on the perceived complexity and effort required to complete a user story relative to other stories. It's a comparative measure rather than an absolute one.

- **Team Consensus:** Estimating User Story Points is a collaborative effort involving the entire team. Team members discuss and collectively agree on the points assigned to each user story, fostering a shared understanding of the work.

- **Fibonacci Sequence:** Teams often use the Fibonacci sequence (1, 2, 3, 5, 8, 13, etc.) for Story Point estimation. The gaps between numbers reflect the uncertainty inherent in larger tasks, acknowledging that estimating larger tasks precisely becomes increasingly challenging.

- **Focus on Effort, Not Time:** User Story Points are a measure of effort, emphasizing the team's perception of the work's complexity. They intentionally avoid the constraints and variability associated with time-based estimates.

Sprint Velocity

Sprint Velocity is a metric used in Scrum to measure the amount of work a team can complete in a single sprint. It represents the total number of User Story Points or other backlog items that a team successfully delivers during a sprint. Sprint Velocity is a key indicator of a team's capacity and helps in planning future sprints by providing insights into the team's historical performance.

Key Characteristics of Sprint Velocity

- **Measuring Capacity:** Sprint Velocity quantifies a team's capacity to complete work within a specific timeframe. It reflects the team's historical ability to deliver a certain amount of work and is often averaged over several sprints for a more accurate representation.
- **Consistency and Predictability:** By tracking Sprint Velocity over multiple sprints, teams can identify patterns and trends. Consistent Sprint Velocities contribute to predictability, helping teams and stakeholders plan future releases with greater confidence.
- **Adaptable:** Sprint Velocity is adaptable and reflects changes in a team's capability over time. If a team undergoes changes in composition, adopts

new tools, or improves its processes, Sprint Velocity can adjust accordingly.

- **Focus on Deliverable Work:** Sprint Velocity is not concerned with the number of tasks started or in progress but focuses on completed and potentially shippable work. It reflects the tangible value delivered by the team at the end of each sprint.

The Interplay Between User Story Points and Sprint Velocity

- **Capacity Planning:** User Story Points aid in capacity planning by helping teams estimate the effort required for upcoming work. Sprint Velocity, in turn, guides teams in determining how many User Story Points they can commit to completing in the next sprint.

- **Relative Estimation:** The use of User Story Points allows teams to estimate the size of tasks relative to one another. This relativity provides a more straightforward way to compare and prioritize user stories during sprint planning.

- **Tracking Progress:** Sprint Velocity serves as a valuable metric for tracking a team's progress. It provides a clear indication of how much work the team can handle in a given sprint, allowing for adjustments as needed.

- **Continuous Improvement:** User Story Points and Sprint Velocity contribute to the principle of continuous improvement in Scrum. Teams can analyze historical data, identify areas for improvement, and adapt their processes to enhance efficiency and effectiveness.

Challenges and Considerations

- **Consistency in Estimation:** Ensuring consistency in User Story Point estimation can be a challenge, especially if team members have different interpretations of complexity. Regular refinement sessions and training can help address this issue.

- **External Influences:** Sprint Velocity may be influenced by external factors such as team composition changes, technology shifts, or unexpected challenges. Teams should be aware of these factors when interpreting Sprint Velocity trends.

- **Avoiding Overemphasis:** While User Story Points and Sprint Velocity are valuable tools, they should not be overemphasized to the detriment of other Agile principles. Teams should prioritize collaboration, adaptability, and delivering value over rigid adherence to metrics.

Summary

User Story Points and Sprint Velocity are integral components of Scrum, offering teams a structured approach to estimating, planning, and tracking progress. By focusing on the relative complexity of tasks and measuring the team's capacity to deliver work, these concepts contribute to the agility, transparency, and predictability of Scrum teams. As organizations continue to embrace Agile methodologies, mastering the art of User Story Points and Sprint Velocity becomes a key factor in achieving successful and sustainable project outcomes.

CHAPTER TWENTY

What are Burn-down and Burn-up charts

What are Burn-down and Burn-up charts

Agile methodologies have revolutionized the landscape of product development, emphasizing flexibility, collaboration, and iterative progress. Two visual tools integral to tracking and communicating project advancement in Agile are Burn Down and Burn Up charts. These charts provide a real-time snapshot of work completion, enabling teams and stakeholders to make informed decisions. This chapter explores the concepts of Burn Down and Burn Up charts, their significance, and how they contribute to the success of Agile product development.

Burn Down Charts: Monitoring Work Remaining

A Burn Down Chart is a graphical representation that tracks the progress of work remaining in a project over time. The horizontal axis typically represents time, divided into iterations or sprints, while the vertical axis represents the amount of work remaining. As the project progresses, the chart "burns down" as work is completed.

Components of a Burn Down Chart

- **Ideal Progress Line:** The ideal progress line represents the rate at which work should be completed for the project to finish on time. It is a straight line connecting the total amount of work at the beginning of the project to zero at the end.

- **Actual Progress Line:** The actual progress line shows the cumulative work completed at each time interval. It provides a visual indication of whether the team is ahead, behind, or on track with the ideal progress line.

- **Remaining Work:** The remaining work is represented as a downward-sloping line on the chart. The steeper the line, the faster the team is completing work. The goal is for this line to meet the x-axis (zero work remaining) by the end of the project.

Interpretation of a Burn Down Chart

- **Ideal vs. Actual Progress:** If the actual progress line closely aligns with the ideal progress line, the team is on track. Deviations between the two lines indicate that the project is ahead or behind schedule.

- **Rate of Progress:** The steepness of the remaining work line provides insights into the team's velocity. A steep line suggests rapid progress, while a flatter line may indicate slower progress.

- **Adjustments and Adaptations:** Teams can use Burn Down Charts to identify trends and patterns. If the chart shows unexpected delays or accelerations, the team can adjust strategies, address impediments, and adapt their approach to meet project goals.

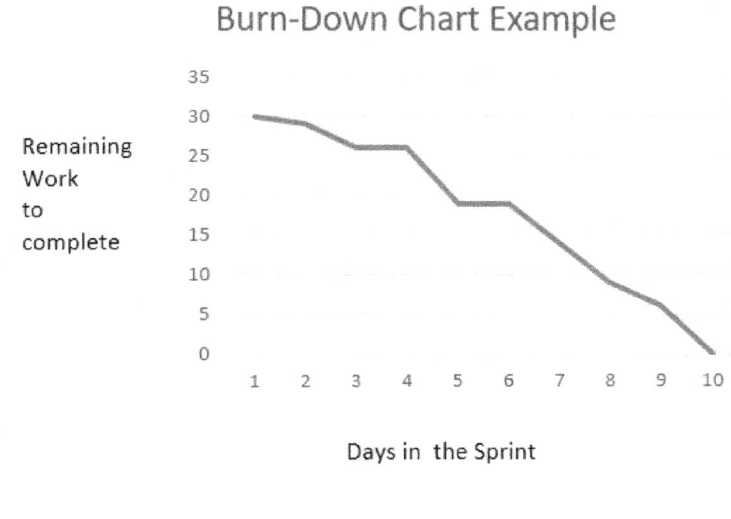

Burn-down Chart Example

Burn Up Charts: Visualizing Total Accomplishment

A Burn Up Chart is another visual tool that tracks and communicates progress in Agile development. Unlike the Burn Down Chart, the Burn Up Chart represents both completed and remaining work, offering a holistic view of total accomplishment throughout the project.

Components of a Burn Up Chart

- **Total Scope Line:** The total scope line represents the entire scope of the project. It is a flat line that extends from the start of the project to the end, indicating the total amount of work to be done.

- **Completed Work Line:** The completed work line shows the cumulative work completed at each time interval. As the team progresses, this line moves upward, illustrating the total amount of work accomplished.

- **Remaining Work:** Similar to the Burn Down Chart, the Burn Up Chart also includes a line representing remaining work. This line typically starts at zero and increases over time.

Interpretation of a Burn Up Chart

- **Total Accomplishment:** The Burn Up Chart provides a clear visual of both completed and remaining work. Stakeholders can easily see the total accomplishment over the course of the project.

- **Rate of Completion:** Analyzing the slope of the completed work line helps stakeholders understand the team's rate of completion. A steeper line suggests faster progress, while a flatter line indicates a slower pace.

- **Scope Adjustments:** Teams can use Burn Up Charts to discuss scope adjustments. If the scope line needs to be expanded or reduced, stakeholders can visually assess the impact on the project's overall progress.

Best Practices for Burn Down and Burn Up Charts

- **Regular Updates:** Both Burn Down and Burn Up Charts should be updated regularly, preferably at the end of each iteration or sprint. This ensures that stakeholders have real-time insights into project progress.

- **Clear and Consistent Definitions:** Define and communicate the metrics used in the charts clearly. Whether measuring story points, tasks, or other units, consistency in definitions enhances the reliability of the charts.

- **Transparency and Collaboration:** Share the charts with the entire team and stakeholders to promote transparency and collaboration. Open discussions about progress, impediments, and adaptations are crucial for success.

- **Data-Driven Decision-Making:** Use the charts as a basis for data-driven decision-making. If the charts indicate deviations from the plan, teams and stakeholders can collaboratively identify solutions and make informed adjustments.

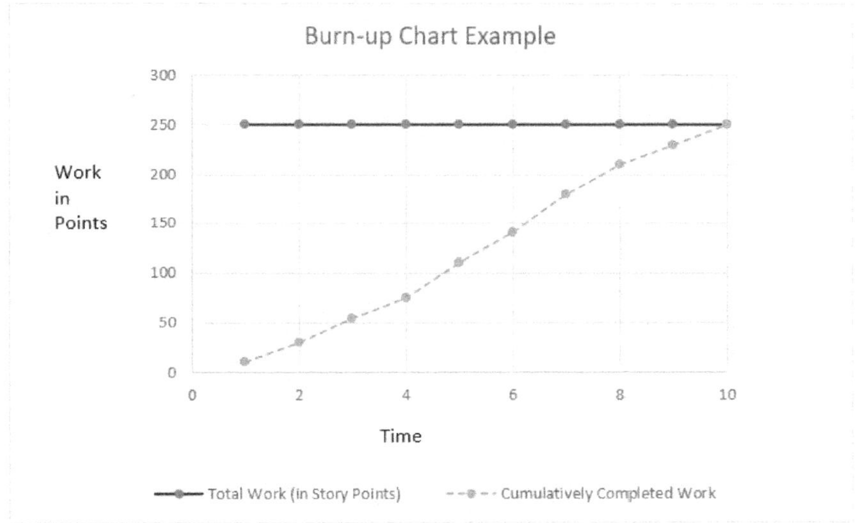

Burn-up Chart Example

Summary

Burn Down and Burn Up Charts are invaluable tools in the Agile practitioner's toolkit, providing a visual representation of project progress that is easily understood by teams and stakeholders alike. Whether monitoring work remaining with a Burn Down Chart or visualizing total accomplishment with a Burn Up Chart, these tools empower teams to adapt, communicate effectively, and navigate the complexities of Agile product development. As organizations continue to embrace Agile methodologies, mastery of these charts becomes essential for fostering collaboration, making informed decisions, and ultimately delivering successful and value-driven projects.

CHAPTER TWENTY-ONE

Transformation: Project Manager to Product Owner

In the evolving landscape of project management, the role of a Product Owner has gained prominence in agile methodologies. For a traditional Project Manager looking to make this transition, it represents not just a change in title but a shift in mindset and responsibilities. This chapter explores the transformation journey from a Project Manager to a Product Owner, unraveling the skills required to excel in the dynamic realm of modern agile management.

Understanding the Mindset Shift

- **Project Manager Mindset:** Traditional project management often revolves around strict adherence to plans, schedules, and deliverables. The focus is on completing tasks and following a predetermined project plan.

- **Product Owner Mindset:** A Product Owner, on the other hand, embraces a customer-centric mindset. Their primary concern is not just delivering features but maximizing the value delivered to the end-users. The Product Owner becomes the voice of the customer within the development team.

Embracing Customer-Centricity

- **Customer Focus:** A great Product Owner understands the customer's needs, preferences, and pain points. This requires active engagement with stakeholders, gathering feedback, and having a deep understanding of the market and user expectations.

- **Market Awareness:** Unlike a Project Manager who may focus on internal project requirements, a Product Owner must keep a pulse on market trends, competitive landscapes, and emerging opportunities to inform product decisions.

Effective Communication Skills

- **Stakeholder Collaboration:** While both roles require communication skills, a Product Owner's communication extends beyond project updates. They must articulate the product vision, goals, and priorities to both internal teams and external stakeholders.

- **Influencing Without Authority:** A Product Owner often needs to influence decisions without direct authority. Persuasion and negotiation skills become crucial in aligning diverse stakeholders toward a common vision.

Prioritization and Value Maximization

- **Value-Driven Decision-Making:** The Product Owner is responsible for prioritizing features based on their value to the end-user and the business. This involves constant evaluation of trade-offs and making decisions that maximize overall product value.

- **Return on Investment (ROI):** Unlike a Project Manager who may focus on on-time and on-budget delivery, a Product Owner assesses the return on investment for each product increment, ensuring that efforts align with strategic business goals.

Deep Product Knowledge

- **Domain Expertise:** A Product Owner should have a profound understanding of the product, its features, and the industry in which it operates. This knowledge is essential for making informed decisions and providing guidance to the development team.

- **Continuous Learning:** Staying abreast of industry trends, user behaviors, and technological advancements is a continuous process for a Product Owner. This adaptability ensures that the product remains competitive and relevant.

Agile Methodology Mastery

- **Scrum and Agile Frameworks:** A successful Product Owner must be well-versed in agile methodologies, particularly Scrum. Understanding the principles of iterative development, sprint planning, and backlog management is fundamental to the role.

- **Empowering Teams:** Unlike a Project Manager who may direct the team, a Product Owner empowers the development team to self-organize and make decisions. Collaboration and trust-building are essential to fostering a high-performing team.

Risk Management and Adaptability

- **Risk Mitigation:** While risk management is a common aspect of both roles, a Product Owner focuses on mitigating risks related to product success. This includes validating assumptions through prototypes, early releases, and continuous feedback loops.

- **Adapting to Change:** Agile environments embrace change, and a Product Owner must be comfortable adapting plans based on evolving requirements, market dynamics, or stakeholder feedback.

Data-Driven Decision-Making

- **Metrics and Analytics:** A Product Owner relies on data to inform decisions. Understanding key performance indicators (KPIs), user analytics, and market data is crucial for making informed choices and iterating on the product strategy.

- **Iterative Improvement:** Regularly reviewing and analyzing metrics allows a Product Owner to iteratively improve the product. This data-driven approach ensures that decisions are grounded in evidence rather than assumptions.

Summary

The transition from a traditional Project Manager to a Product Owner is a transformative journey that requires not only acquiring new skills but also adopting a fundamentally different mindset. The shift from a focus on tasks and timelines to a customer-centric, value-driven approach is at the core of this evolution. Success in the role of a Product Owner hinges on effective communication, prioritization based on value, continuous learning, and the ability to navigate the dynamic landscape of agile methodologies. As organizations increasingly embrace agile practices, the Product Owner role becomes a linchpin for delivering products that not only meet expectations but exceed them, ensuring long-term success in the ever-evolving world of modern agile management.

CHAPTER TWENTY-TWO

Product Owner vs Product Manager

In the dynamic realm of product development, the roles of Product Owner and Product Manager are often crucial to the success of a product. While the terms are sometimes used interchangeably, they represent distinct roles with unique responsibilities. This chapter aims to provide a detailed exploration of the differences between the Product Owner and Product Manager roles, shedding light on their respective functions, focus areas, and contributions to the overall product lifecycle.

Product Owner

The Product Owner is a key role within the Agile framework, primarily associated with Scrum methodology. This individual acts as a bridge between the development team and stakeholders, ensuring that the product backlog is well-defined, prioritized, and aligned with the overall vision.

Key Responsibilities of Product Owner

- **Backlog Management:** The Product Owner is responsible for creating and maintaining the product backlog, a dynamic list of features, enhancements, and bug fixes. This involves prioritizing items based on value and ensuring that the team works on the most valuable tasks first.

- **User Stories:** Crafting user stories, which are concise, customer-centric descriptions of functionality, is a core responsibility. The Product Owner ensures that user stories are clear, actionable, and aligned with user needs and business objectives.

- **Prioritization:** Prioritizing features and tasks is a crucial aspect of the Product Owner's role. This involves considering factors such as customer feedback, market trends, and business priorities to make informed decisions about what should be worked on next.

- **Acceptance Criteria:** Defining acceptance criteria for user stories is essential for effective communication between the development team and stakeholders. The Product Owner specifies the conditions that must be met for a user story to be considered complete.

- **Continuous Feedback:** The Product Owner gathers continuous feedback from stakeholders, customers, and the development team. This feedback loop helps in refining and adjusting priorities based on changing requirements and market conditions.

Product Manager

The Product Manager is a broader role that encompasses various aspects of the product lifecycle, from ideation to delivery. While the Product Owner is often associated with Agile methodologies, the Product Manager operates in both Agile and non-Agile environments, playing a strategic role in product development.

Key Responsibilities of Product Manager

- **Market Research and Strategy:** Product Managers conduct market research to understand customer needs, industry trends, and competitive landscapes. They define the product strategy, aligning it with the organization's overall goals and objectives.

- **Roadmap Planning:** Developing and communicating the product roadmap is a key responsibility. The Product Manager outlines the high-level plan for product development, indicating major milestones, feature releases, and strategic initiatives.

- **Cross-Functional Collaboration:** Product Managers collaborate with various teams, including development, marketing, sales, and customer support. They act as a central point of communication, ensuring that all teams are aligned with the product strategy and vision.

- **Go-to-Market Strategy:** Planning the go-to-market strategy for product launches is a critical aspect of the Product Manager's role. This involves coordinating with marketing and sales teams to ensure a successful product introduction to the market.

- **Financial Management:** Product Managers often have financial responsibilities, including budgeting, forecasting, and ensuring that the product operates within financial constraints. They must make decisions that align with the organization's financial objectives.

So, what are the Key Differences ?

PO vs PM

a) Scope of Responsibility

- **Product Owner:** The Product Owner's responsibilities are primarily focused on the Agile development process. Their scope is narrower, concentrating on backlog management, user stories, and ensuring the development team delivers value incrementally.

- **Product Manager:** Product Managers have a broader scope that extends across the entire product lifecycle. They are involved in strategic planning, market analysis, and collaboration with various departments to ensure the overall success of the product.

b) *Strategic vs Tactical Focus*

- **Product Owner:** The Product Owner's focus is more tactical, dealing with day-to-day activities of the development team. Their primary concern is delivering incremental value through the product backlog and user stories.

- **Product Manager:** Product Managers take a strategic approach, considering the long-term vision for the product. They are concerned with the market, competition, and how the product aligns with the organization's business goals.

c) *Stakeholder Interaction*

- **Product Owner:** The primary stakeholders for the Product Owner are the development team and product stakeholders involved in the Agile process. They work closely with these groups to ensure effective communication and feedback.

- **Product Manager:** Product Managers interact with a broader range of stakeholders, including executives, marketing teams, sales teams, and customer support. They need to align the product strategy with the interests and goals of various departments.

d) *Agile vs Non-Agile Environments*

- **Product Owner:** The role of Product Owner is closely associated with Agile methodologies, particularly Scrum. They operate within the framework of Agile ceremonies and principles.

- **Product Manager:** Product Managers work in both Agile and non-Agile environments. They adapt their approach based on the organizational structure and methodologies in place.

Collaboration between Product Owner and Product Manager

While these roles have distinct responsibilities, successful product development often requires a close collaboration between Product Owners and Product Managers. The two roles complement each other, with the Product Manager providing the strategic vision and the Product Owner ensuring that the vision is realized through day-to-day execution.

- **Communication:** Regular communication between the Product Owner and Product Manager is essential. This ensures alignment between strategic goals and the work being done by the development team.

- **Feedback Loop:** The Product Owner provides valuable feedback to the Product Manager based on the realities of the development process. This feedback loop helps in refining the product strategy and roadmap.

- **Prioritization:** While the Product Owner focuses on prioritizing tasks within the development team, collaboration with the Product Manager ensures that these priorities align with the broader product strategy.

- **Strategic Alignment:** Product Managers and Product Owners work together to ensure that the tactical decisions made by the Product Owner align with the overall strategic goals set by the Product Manager.

Summary

In the intricate landscape of product development, both the Product Owner and Product Manager play pivotal roles, each contributing to the success of a product in its own way. Understanding the distinctions between these roles is essential for organizations seeking to build effective and cohesive product teams. By recognizing the unique responsibilities and focus areas of Product Owners and Product Managers, organizations can create a harmonious and productive environment that drives innovation, aligns with strategic goals, and ultimately delivers successful products to the market.

CHAPTER TWENTY-THREE

Transformation: Business Analyst to Product Owner

Transformation: Business Analyst to Product Owner

In the dynamic landscape of product development and project management, the roles of Product Owner and Business Analyst play crucial parts in ensuring the success of a project. However, these roles are distinct, with unique responsibilities and skill sets. In this chapter, we will delve into the key differences between a Product Owner and a Business Analyst, and explore how one can transition from a Business Analyst to a Product Owner.

Differences Between Product Owner and Business Analyst

Focus and Scope:

- **Product Owner:** Primarily concerned with the product and its features. Responsible for maximizing the value of the product and managing the product backlog.

- **Business Analyst:** Focuses on understanding business processes, gathering requirements, and ensuring that the solution meets business needs.

Responsibilities:

- Product Owner: Owns the product vision, prioritizes features, and works closely with stakeholders to define requirements. Ensures the development team delivers high-value features.

- Business Analyst: Analyzes and documents business processes, elicits and documents requirements, and acts as a liaison between business stakeholders and the development team.

Stakeholder Interaction:

- **Product Owner:** Collaborates with stakeholders, including customers, to understand their needs and expectations. Acts as the voice of the customer.

- **Business Analyst:** Engages with a wide range of stakeholders to gather, validate, and document requirements. Acts as a mediator between business and technical teams.

Decision-Making Authority:

- **Product Owner:** Has the authority to make decisions on prioritization and features to be developed. Acts as the final decision-maker for the product.

- **Business Analyst:** Facilitates decision-making by providing analysis and insights but typically does not have the final say on project priorities.

Timeline and Iterations:

- **Product Owner:** Works in iterative cycles (e.g., Agile) and is responsible for ensuring that the team delivers a potentially shippable product increment at the end of each iteration.

- **Business Analyst:** May work on projects with different methodologies, and the focus is often on the overall project timeline and milestones.

Transitioning from Business Analyst to Product Owner

- **Understand the Product Owner Role:** Gain a deep understanding of the responsibilities and expectations of a Product Owner, including the ability to make decisions and prioritize effectively.

- **Develop Stakeholder Management Skills:** Strengthen communication and relationship-building skills to effectively collaborate with stakeholders and represent their needs in the product development process.

- **Learn Agile and Scrum Methodologies:** Familiarize yourself with Agile principles and Scrum practices, as many Product Owner roles operate within these frameworks.

- **Enhance Decision-Making Abilities:** Cultivate the ability to make informed decisions based on business priorities, customer feedback, and project constraints.

- **Expand Technical Knowledge:** While not mandatory, having a basic understanding of the technical aspects of the product and development process can be beneficial for effective collaboration with the development team.

- **Demonstrate Leadership:** Showcase leadership qualities by taking initiative, being proactive, and demonstrating a strong sense of ownership over the product.

- **Build a Product Mindset:** Shift your mindset from a project-oriented perspective to a product-oriented one. Understand the long-term vision and goals for the product.

Summary

In conclusion, while the roles of Product Owner and Business Analyst share some commonalities, they are distinct in their focus, responsibilities, and decision-making authority. Transitioning from a Business Analyst to a Product Owner requires a deliberate effort to acquire the necessary skills, knowledge, and mindset. By understanding the key differences and proactively developing the relevant competencies, individuals can successfully navigate this transition and contribute to the success of product development initiatives.

CHAPTER TWENTY-FOUR

Achieving Technical Agility

In today's fast-paced and dynamic business environment, the ability to respond quickly to changing market demands is crucial for the success of any software development project. Technical agility, the capability to rapidly adapt to evolving technical requirements and deliver high-quality software, has become a key focus for agile teams. This chapter explores how implementing practices such as Continuous Integration/Continuous Deployment (CI/CD), Test Automation, DevOps, and Microservices Architecture can empower agile teams to achieve unparalleled levels of technical agility.

Continuous Integration/Continuous Deployment (CI/CD)

CI/CD is a set of practices that allow development teams to automate the building, testing, and deployment of code changes. By integrating code changes frequently, teams can identify and address issues early in the development process, leading to a more stable and reliable codebase.

Benefits of CI/CD:

- **Faster Time to Market:** CI/CD streamlines the development pipeline, reducing the time it takes to turn code changes into production-ready releases.

- **Early Detection of Issues:** Automated testing in the CI/CD pipeline enables early detection of bugs and other issues, preventing them from reaching the production environment.

- **Consistent and Reliable Builds:** Automation ensures that every build is consistent and reliable, reducing the risk of integration problems.

Test Automation

Test Automation is a critical component of achieving technical agility. Automated testing allows teams to quickly and efficiently verify the functionality, performance, and security of their software, enabling faster and more reliable releases.

Benefits of Test Automation:

- **Rapid Feedback:** Automated tests provide rapid feedback to developers, allowing them to identify and fix issues as soon as they arise.

- **Regression Testing:** Automated tests ensure that existing functionalities remain intact when new features are added or modifications are made, preventing regression issues.

- **Increased Test Coverage:** Automated tests can cover a broad range of scenarios, including edge cases and performance testing, improving overall software quality.

DevOps

DevOps is a cultural and collaborative approach that integrates development and operations teams. It emphasizes automation, communication, and shared responsibilities, enabling faster and more reliable software delivery.

Benefits of DevOps:

- **Improved Collaboration:** DevOps breaks down silos between development and operations teams, fostering better communication and collaboration.

- **Automated Deployment:** Automated deployment processes ensure consistency and reliability, reducing the likelihood of deployment errors.

- **Continuous Monitoring:** DevOps practices include continuous monitoring, allowing teams to identify and address issues in real-time.

Microservices Architecture

Microservices Architecture is an architectural style that structures an application as a collection of loosely coupled, independently deployable services. This approach enhances scalability, flexibility, and maintainability.

Benefits of Microservices Architecture:

- **Scalability:** Microservices can be independently scaled, allowing teams to scale specific components based on demand.

- **Fault Isolation:** Isolating services reduces the impact of failures, ensuring that a failure in one service does not bring down the entire application.

- **Technology Flexibility:** Microservices allow teams to choose the best technology stack for each service, promoting flexibility and innovation.

Summary

Achieving technical agility in agile teams requires a holistic approach that encompasses CI/CD, Test Automation, DevOps, and Microservices Architecture. These practices collectively empower teams to respond rapidly to changing requirements, deliver high-quality software, and maintain a competitive edge in today's fast-paced business landscape. By adopting these principles, agile teams can build a foundation for continuous improvement, innovation, and successful software delivery.

The Global Need for Scrum Masters

As organizations worldwide embark on the Agile journey, the role of Scrum Masters has taken center stage in the realm of IT project management. The question of how many Scrum Masters are needed in the IT world has become a pivotal one, shaping the dynamics of modern Agile teams. In this comprehensive exploration, we delve into the multifaceted aspects of this query, addressing the varying needs, roles, and structures that determine the global demand for Scrum Masters.

The Agile Revolution

Around three years ago, a prediction surfaced in my mind that every traditional IT team would transform into a Scrum Team within next five years. Looking at the current job landscape filled with opportunities for Agile roles such as Agile Coach, Scrum Master, Product Owner, and Product Manager across thousands of organizations globally, it's evident that "Agile" has become the predominant mantra for modern teams and projects.

The Pervasiveness of Scrum

Among the various Agile frameworks, Scrum stands out as the most widely used. Integrated with other methodologies like Systems Thinking, Lean, Kanban, Extreme Programming, Scaled Agile Framework (SAFe), and Disciplined Agile Development (DAD), Scrum plays a pivotal role in helping teams achieve agility. At its core, Scrum involves three key roles: Scrum Master, Product Owner, and Team.

Quantifying the Need

The heart of the matter lies in understanding how many Scrum Masters are needed in the IT world. To answer this, it's crucial to evaluate how many Scrum teams an organization can form. As companies transition from traditional teams to Agile Scrum Teams, the integration of Scrum into various Agile methodologies becomes essential, resulting in the need for a Scrum Master for every modern Agile Scrum Team.

Partial Scrum Masters

Some teams opt for Partial Scrum Masters, wherein one of the team members takes on the dual role of an individual contributor (IC) and Scrum Master. While this approach can work effectively for teams not part of any Release Train or Tribe, challenges may arise. Partial Scrum Masters might experience burnout due to limited empowerment, challenges in balancing roles, and potential disengagement from the team.

Project Managers as Scrum Masters

In certain scenarios, organizations assign their Project Managers as Scrum Masters. This approach, however, has a lower success rate as traditional control-based managers may struggle to adapt to the modern Agile model, which emphasizes Servant Leadership. While some project managers may succeed as Scrum Masters, the overall success rate in this model is relatively low.

The Full-Time Scrum Master Model

As organizations recognize the need for dedicated Scrum Masters, the concept of full-time Scrum Masters gains prominence. In many cases, organizations assign 2 or 3 Scrum Teams to each Full-Time Scrum Master. It's noteworthy that whether full-time or partial, Scrum Masters do not have direct reports. This model is particularly effective when Scrum Teams are part of a larger system, such as Release Trains or Tribes.

Determining the Numbers

For organizations with 100 Scrum Teams, the need for approximately 30 to 40 Scrum Masters arises, based on the complexity of their products and projects. The allocation of 2 or 3 Scrum Teams to a Full-Time Scrum Master becomes a strategic approach to achieving and maintaining agility within larger systems.

Summary

In conclusion, the demand for Scrum Masters is escalating globally as organizations commit to Agile transformations. The modern IT world requires more Scrum Masters to provide the essential Servant Leadership that fuels Agile success. Every Agile team needs a Scrum Master, and the optimal approach involves assigning 2 or 3 Scrum Teams to a Full-Time Scrum Master. As organizations navigate the Agile landscape, recognizing the significance of Scrum Masters in achieving and sustaining agility is paramount to their success in the dynamic realm of IT project management and product development.

CHAPTER TWENTY-SIX

Transformation: Project Manager to Scrum Master

Transformation: Project Manager to Scrum Master

As organizations shift towards agile methodologies, the role of a Scrum Master has emerged as a linchpin in fostering collaboration, adaptability, and continuous improvement. For a traditional Project Manager seeking to make this transition, it's not just a change in title but a shift in responsibilities and mindset. This chapter delves into the journey of transforming from a Project Manager to a Scrum Master, providing the essential skills required to excel in the dynamic landscape of modern agile management.

Understanding the Agile Mindset

- **Project Manager Mindset:** Traditional project management often revolves around detailed planning, strict timelines, and a focus on completing tasks. The Project Manager is a central figure directing the team towards project goals.

- **Scrum Master Mindset:** A Scrum Master, on the other hand, operates from a servant-leadership perspective. The focus is on facilitating and enabling the Scrum Team to self-organize, collaborate, and continuously improve.

Servant Leadership and Facilitation

- **Facilitator Role:** A Scrum Master acts as a facilitator, removing impediments and fostering an environment where the team can thrive. This requires a shift from a directive leadership style to one that supports and serves the team.

- **Empowering Teams:** Unlike a Project Manager who may assign tasks, a Scrum Master empowers the team to take ownership of their work. This involves guiding the team towards self-organization and decision-making.

Effective Communication and Collaboration

- **Collaborative Approach:** A Scrum Master emphasizes collaboration over command and control. Strong interpersonal and communication skills are crucial for facilitating discussions, resolving conflicts, and ensuring transparent communication within the team.

- **Active Listening:** The ability to actively listen to team members and stakeholders is a key aspect of the Scrum Master role. Understanding concerns, challenges, and feedback contributes to a more responsive and adaptive team environment.

Agile Methodology Mastery

- **Scrum Framework Expertise:** A successful Scrum Master should have a deep understanding of the Scrum framework, including roles, events, and artifacts. Mastery of agile principles, such as iterative development and continuous improvement, is fundamental to the role.

- **Adaptability to Change:** Agile environments embrace change, and a Scrum Master must guide the team in adapting to evolving requirements, priorities, and feedback. This requires flexibility and an openness to change.

Conflict Resolution and Emotional Intelligence

- **Conflict Resolution:** In the collaborative environment of agile teams, conflicts may arise. A Scrum Master must be adept at resolving conflicts amicably, promoting a positive team culture.

- **Emotional Intelligence:** Understanding and managing one's emotions and those of others is a key aspect of emotional intelligence. This skill is invaluable for building strong team dynamics and fostering a positive work environment.

Continuous Improvement and Kaizen Mindset

- **Kaizen Philosophy:** The Scrum Master role is deeply tied to the philosophy of continuous improvement. Encouraging the team to reflect on their processes, identify areas for improvement, and implement changes is crucial for enhancing overall efficiency.

- **Iterative Feedback Loops:** Establishing regular feedback loops, such as sprint retrospectives, enables the team to reflect on their performance and make iterative improvements. A Scrum Master facilitates these sessions to drive continuous learning.

Stakeholder Management

- **Stakeholder Collaboration:** While a Project Manager may primarily interact with stakeholders on project progress, a Scrum Master involves stakeholders in the agile process. This requires effective communication and collaboration with both internal and external stakeholders.

- **Transparency and Visibility:** Ensuring transparency in the team's work and providing visibility into progress are critical aspects of stakeholder management. A Scrum Master facilitates communication channels to keep stakeholders informed.

Courage and Assertiveness

- **Courageous Leadership:** A Scrum Master needs the courage to challenge the status quo, advocate for agile principles, and protect the team from external disruptions. This requires assertiveness and a commitment to the team's well-being.

- **Serving as a Shield:** Shielding the team from external pressures and interruptions is a key responsibility. A Scrum Master must be assertive in safeguarding the team's focus and ensuring they have the environment needed for success.

Summary

The transition from a traditional Project Manager to a Scrum Master is a transformative journey that requires not only acquiring new skills but adopting a fundamentally different mindset. Success in the role of a Scrum Master hinges on servant leadership, effective communication, collaboration, and a commitment to continuous improvement. As organizations increasingly embrace agile methodologies, the Scrum Master becomes a catalyst for fostering high-performing teams, adapting to change, and delivering value iteratively. The journey from Project Manager to Scrum Master is not just a professional evolution; it's an opportunity to contribute to a culture of agility, innovation, and collaboration in the dynamic landscape of modern agile management.

CHAPTER TWENTY-SEVEN

Change Management for Agile Transformation

Change is a constant in the dynamic world of business, and Agile Transformation represents a significant shift in how organizations approach work, collaboration, and value delivery. However, introducing Agile practices involves more than just altering processes—it requires a thoughtful and strategic approach to Change Management. This chapter delves into the concept of Change Management, its importance in the context of Agile Transformation, and practical steps for successful implementation.

Understanding Change Management

Change Management is a structured approach to transitioning individuals, teams, and organizations from their current state to a desired future state. It involves planning, executing, and reinforcing changes to processes, systems, and behaviors to achieve positive outcomes and minimize resistance. In the context of Agile Transformation, Change Management becomes a crucial enabler for fostering a culture of agility, adaptability, and collaboration.

Key Components

- **Vision and Strategy:** Clearly articulate the vision and strategy behind the Agile Transformation. Communicate the reasons for change, the desired outcomes, and the benefits of embracing Agile principles.

- **Stakeholder Engagement:** Identify and engage key stakeholders at all levels of the organization. This includes leadership, teams, and individuals impacted by the transformation. Establish open channels of communication to address concerns and gather feedback.

- **Communication Planning:** Develop a comprehensive communication plan. Keep stakeholders informed about the Agile Transformation journey, milestones, and changes to processes. Consistent and transparent communication is essential for building understanding and trust.

- **Training and Skill Development:** Provide training and support to help individuals and teams acquire the necessary skills for Agile practices. This may include workshops, coaching, and resources to ensure a smooth transition to the Agile way of working.

- **Change Metrics and Monitoring:** Define key metrics to measure the success of the Agile Transformation. Regularly monitor and evaluate progress, seeking feedback from teams and stakeholders. Use data to make informed decisions and adjust the transformation approach as needed.

Implementing Change Management for Agile Transformation

1. **Establish a Compelling Vision:** Define a clear and compelling vision for the Agile Transformation. This vision should articulate the desired outcomes, benefits, and the positive impact on the organization. Ensure that the vision is communicated consistently across all levels of the organization.
2. **Secure Leadership Buy-In:** Obtain buy-in and commitment from organizational leaders. Leadership support is crucial for overcoming resistance and demonstrating the importance of the Agile Transformation. Leaders should actively communicate their support, participate in training, and model Agile behaviors.

3. **Build a Change Coalition:** Assemble a change coalition or steering committee representing various stakeholders. This group plays a pivotal role in driving the transformation, aligning efforts, and addressing challenges. Include representatives from different departments and levels of the organization.

4. **Assess Organizational Readiness:** Conduct a thorough assessment of the organization's readiness for Agile Transformation. This includes evaluating existing processes, culture, and the level of familiarity with Agile principles. Identify potential challenges and areas that require targeted interventions.

5. **Develop a Comprehensive Communication Plan:** Craft a communication plan that addresses the "why," "what," and "how" of the Agile Transformation. Tailor communication to different audiences and channels, ensuring that information is disseminated consistently and transparently. Use a variety of mediums, such as town halls, newsletters, and workshops.

6. **Provide Agile Training and Support:** Offer Agile training programs for individuals and teams. These programs should cover Agile principles, frameworks (e.g., Scrum, Kanban), and the specific practices relevant to the organization. Support training with coaching and mentoring to reinforce learning and address real-world challenges.

7. **Foster a Culture of Collaboration:** Encourage a culture of collaboration and continuous improvement. Create opportunities for cross-functional teams to work together, share insights, and learn from one another. Recognize and celebrate achievements to reinforce the positive aspects of the Agile mindset.

8. **Empower Teams and Individuals:** Empower teams to make decisions and take ownership of their work. Create an environment that values autonomy, accountability, and experimentation. Encourage individuals to contribute their ideas, and recognize and reward innovative and collaborative behavior.

9. **Monitor and Adjust:** Regularly monitor the progress of the Agile Transformation. Use feedback mechanisms, surveys, and key performance indicators (KPIs) to assess the impact on teams and the organization. Be prepared to make adjustments to the transformation approach based on real-time insights.

10. **Sustain and Scale:** Ensure that Agile practices are sustained over time and integrated into the organization's DNA. Look for opportunities to

scale Agile practices to other parts of the organization, creating a ripple effect of agility and adaptability.

Challenges and Considerations

- **Resistance to Change:** Anticipate and address resistance to change. Engage with individuals early in the process, listen to their concerns, and involve them in the decision-making process.

- **Cultural Misalignment:** Recognize and address cultural misalignments that may hinder the Agile Transformation. Align Agile values with the organization's existing culture, and promote cultural shifts that support agility.

- **Overcoming Legacy Processes:** Overcoming entrenched legacy processes can be a challenge. Identify areas where existing processes may hinder agility and work collaboratively to adapt or replace them.

- **Measuring Success:** Define clear success criteria for the Agile Transformation. This may include improvements in delivery speed, customer satisfaction, and the ability to respond to market changes. Regularly assess progress against these criteria.

Summary

Implementing Change Management for Agile Transformation is not a one-size-fits-all endeavor; it requires a thoughtful and adaptable approach. By fostering a culture of openness, collaboration, and continuous improvement, organizations can navigate the complexities of change and unlock the full potential of Agile practices. The journey towards an Agile mindset is transformative, and successful Change Management is the compass that guides organizations toward sustainable agility and excellence.

CHAPTER TWENTY-EIGHT

Transformation: Project Manager to Change Agent

In the ever-evolving landscape of modern management, the role of a traditional Project Manager is expanding beyond the confines of project delivery. The demand for adept Change Management professionals has surged as organizations recognize the need for seamless transitions in the face of dynamic markets and evolving technologies. This chapter explores the key steps and skills required for a traditional Project Manager to successfully metamorphose into a Change Management professional in today's business environment.

Understanding the Shift

While project management focuses on delivering a specific outcome within defined constraints, Change Management is concerned with guiding individuals and organizations through transitions. It involves not just implementing new processes or technologies but ensuring that individuals adapt successfully to the changes, minimizing resistance, and maximizing the benefits of the transformation.

Key Steps for Transformation

- **a) Develop a Change Mindset:** Shifting from the project-centric mindset to a change-oriented perspective is the first crucial step. Change Management professionals need to understand the psychology of change, empathy for those impacted, and a deep appreciation for the human side of organizational transformation.

- **b) Cultivate Emotional Intelligence:** Successful Change Managers excel in emotional intelligence. This involves understanding and managing one's emotions and effectively navigating the emotions of others. Empathy, active listening, and strong interpersonal skills become pivotal in guiding individuals through the uncertainties of change.

- **c) Master Communication Strategies:** Communication lies at the heart of Change Management. Change Managers must articulate the vision for change, the reasons behind it, and the benefits that will result. Tailoring messages to different audiences, fostering open dialogue, and addressing concerns are critical components of effective communication in change initiatives.

- **d) Create a Comprehensive Change Plan:** While project managers are accustomed to planning within the constraints of scope, time, and budget, Change Management plans encompass a broader spectrum. A Change Manager must develop a comprehensive plan that addresses communication strategies, stakeholder engagement, training programs, and resistance mitigation.

- **e) Build Stakeholder Engagement:** Stakeholder buy-in is pivotal in change initiatives. Change Managers must identify and engage key stakeholders early in the process, involving them in decision-making and addressing their concerns. Building a coalition of support is essential for the success of any organizational change.

- **f) Implement Change Readiness Assessments:** Unlike traditional project management, Change Management requires continuous assessment of an organization's readiness for change. Change Managers employ tools and methodologies to gauge the readiness of individuals and the organization as a whole, making informed decisions about the pace and scale of the change.

- **g) Facilitate Training and Development:** Change often involves acquiring new skills and adapting to different ways of working. Change Managers play a pivotal role in designing and implementing training programs to equip individuals with the skills required for success in the transformed environment.

- **h) Measure and Evaluate:** While project managers measure success based on the completion of deliverables, Change Managers assess success by the degree of adoption and sustainability of the change. Establishing key performance indicators (KPIs) and regularly evaluating the impact of the change is vital for ongoing success.

Summary

The journey from Project Manager to Change Management professional requires a holistic understanding of organizational dynamics, effective communication strategies, and a deep commitment to the human side of change. By cultivating emotional intelligence, mastering communication, and implementing comprehensive change plans, Project Managers can successfully navigate the intricacies of organizational change in the modern business landscape. The role of a Change Management professional is not just about managing projects; it's about guiding people through the transformative journey toward a more adaptive and resilient organization.

Demystifying Scrum of Scrums

In the dynamic and collaborative realm of Agile development, the Scrum framework has become a cornerstone for managing complex projects. As projects scale in size and involve multiple teams, the need for effective coordination and communication becomes paramount. Enter the "Scrum of Scrums," a scaled Agile technique designed to facilitate collaboration among multiple Scrum teams. This chapter explores the concept of the Scrum of Scrums, its purpose, structure, and best practices for implementation in large-scale Agile projects.

The Essence of Scrum of Scrums

Definition:

The Scrum of Scrums (SoS) is a scaling Agile technique that enables multiple Scrum teams to collaborate and coordinate their efforts to deliver a large-scale project. It serves as a mechanism for sharing information, addressing dependencies, and ensuring alignment among different teams working on interconnected components or features.

Purpose:

The primary purpose of the Scrum of Scrums is to enhance coordination and communication across multiple Scrum teams. As projects grow in complexity and involve interdependent workstreams, the Scrum of Scrums provides a structured way for teams to synchronize their activities, share updates, and collectively address challenges.

Structure and Mechanics

- **Team Composition:** Each Scrum team selects one or more representatives to participate in the Scrum of Scrums. These representatives, often Scrum Masters or team leads, act as liaisons between their respective teams and the larger coordination effort.

- **Frequency:** The Scrum of Scrums typically occurs at a regular cadence, aligned with the overall Scrum events. Depending on the project's needs, it may take place daily, a few times a week, or as determined by the teams.

Meeting Agenda

- **Updates:** Each team representative provides updates on their team's progress, including completed work, work in progress, and any impediments or challenges they are facing.

- **Dependencies:** Teams discuss dependencies and inter-team collaborations. This includes identifying and addressing dependencies, ensuring that work aligns across teams, and resolving any conflicts or overlaps.

- **Impediments:** Representatives share information about impediments or obstacles their teams are encountering. The goal is to collaboratively find solutions and prevent these impediments from hindering overall progress.

- **Planning and Coordination:** Teams discuss upcoming work, align priorities, and coordinate plans to ensure a cohesive approach to achieving project goals. This may involve adjusting sprint backlogs, refining user stories, or synchronizing release plans.

- **Continuous Improvement:** The Scrum of Scrums serves as an opportunity for teams to reflect on their collaborative processes and identify opportunities for improvement. This aligns with the Agile principle of continuous improvement.

Best Practices for Scrum of Scrums

- **Clear Communication:** Effective communication is crucial. Representatives should communicate clearly and concisely, ensuring that information is relayed accurately and understood by all teams.

- **Focus on Dependencies:** Identifying and addressing dependencies is a key aspect of the Scrum of Scrums. Teams should collaboratively work to resolve dependencies and prevent bottlenecks.

- **Timely Updates:** Regular and timely updates are essential. Teams should provide updates on their progress, impediments, and upcoming work to keep everyone informed.

- **Proactive Problem-Solving:** The Scrum of Scrums is a forum for proactive problem-solving. Teams should come prepared to discuss impediments and contribute to finding solutions collaboratively.

- **Shared Ownership:** Teams should cultivate a sense of shared ownership for the overall project. This includes aligning priorities, coordinating plans, and embracing a collective responsibility for project success.

- **Adaptability:** The Agile mindset of adaptability is crucial in the Scrum of Scrums. Teams should be open to adjusting plans, reprioritizing work, and adapting to changing circumstances.

- **Regular Inspections:** The Scrum of Scrums is not a one-time event; it's an ongoing practice. Teams should regularly inspect and adapt their collaboration processes to ensure continuous improvement.

Challenges and Considerations

- **Time Zone Differences:** In globally distributed teams, time zone differences can pose a challenge. Teams should find ways to accommodate different time zones, such as rotating meeting times or leveraging asynchronous communication tools.

- **Information Overload:** With multiple teams providing updates, there's a risk of information overload. Teams should strive to keep updates concise and relevant, focusing on critical information.

- **Dependency Management:** Effectively managing dependencies requires a proactive approach. Teams should establish clear communication channels and mechanisms for identifying and resolving dependencies in a timely manner.

- **Balancing Autonomy and Coordination:** Striking the right balance between team autonomy and coordination is essential. Teams should retain autonomy over their work while actively collaborating to achieve common project goals.

Summary

In the intricate landscape of large-scale Agile development, the Scrum of Scrums emerges as a powerful tool for fostering collaboration and coordination among multiple Scrum teams. By providing a structured forum for communication, updates, and collaborative problem-solving, the Scrum of Scrums empowers teams to navigate complexity, address dependencies, and work collectively toward project success. As organizations continue to embrace Agile principles and scale their projects, mastering the art of the Scrum of Scrums becomes an invaluable skill for ensuring a cohesive and aligned approach to delivering value.

CHAPTER THIRTY

Transformation: Project Manager to Program Manager

In the dynamic landscape of project management, the role of a traditional Project Manager is evolving into that of a Program Management professional. Modern business environments demand a more strategic and holistic approach to managing multiple projects, and Program Management offers the framework needed to navigate these complexities. In this chapter, we will explore the key steps and skills required for a traditional Project Manager to successfully transition into a Program Management role in the contemporary business world.

Understanding the Difference

Before delving into the transformation process, it's crucial to understand the distinctions between project and program management. Project management typically involves overseeing a single initiative with well-defined objectives, scope, and timeline. Program Management, on the other hand, involves the coordination and management of multiple interdependent projects to achieve strategic business goals.

Key Steps for Transformation

- **a) Develop a Strategic Mindset:** Traditional Project Managers are often focused on delivering a specific project within scope, time, and budget.

Program Management requires a broader perspective, involving a strategic mindset to align projects with overarching business objectives. This shift involves understanding organizational goals, market dynamics, and long-term visions.

- **b) Enhance Leadership and Communication Skills:** Effective leadership and communication become even more critical in Program Management. A Program Manager must inspire and lead a team of project managers, fostering collaboration and clear communication channels. Building strong relationships with stakeholders, executives, and team members is key to successful program delivery.

- **c) Master Stakeholder Management:** Program Managers deal with a larger set of stakeholders with diverse interests and expectations. Developing expertise in stakeholder management involves identifying, analyzing, and engaging stakeholders at different levels. This includes maintaining transparent communication and managing conflicts effectively.

- **d) Embrace Change Management:** Programs often involve significant organizational change. Program Managers must be adept at change management principles to navigate and guide teams through transitions. This requires a keen understanding of how changes impact individuals and the organization as a whole.

- **e) Risk Management on a Program Level:** While project managers focus on mitigating risks within the confines of their projects, Program Managers must assess and manage risks across multiple projects. This involves developing a comprehensive risk management strategy that considers the interdependencies between projects and their impact on the program as a whole.

- **f) Implement Robust Governance:** Establishing governance structures is crucial for effective Program Management. This includes defining roles and responsibilities, creating reporting mechanisms, and ensuring accountability across the program. Governance provides the necessary framework for decision-making and ensures alignment with organizational objectives.

- **g) Utilize Technology and Tools:** The modern Program Manager leverages advanced project and program management tools to enhance efficiency and collaboration. Familiarity with tools such as portfolio management software, collaboration platforms, and data analytics can significantly improve program outcomes.

- **h) Continuous Learning and Adaptation:** The evolution from Project Manager to Program Management professional is an ongoing process. Continuous learning, staying updated on industry best practices, and adapting to new methodologies are essential for success in this dynamic field.

Summary

The transition from traditional Project Management to Program Management requires a shift in mindset, skills, and approaches. Embracing a strategic outlook, leadership and communication skills, mastering stakeholder management, and adopting modern tools are integral components of this transformation. By undertaking these steps, Project Managers can successfully navigate the complexities of program management in the modern business landscape, contributing to the overall success of their organizations.

Beyond the Projects: Agile Management

Agile management, born out of the necessity for flexible and adaptive approaches in software development, has transcended its origins and evolved into a comprehensive management philosophy that extends far beyond the confines of traditional project management. In contrast to the linear and structured nature of project management methodologies, Agile embraces change, collaboration, and continuous improvement, making it a transformative force across various organizational domains. This chapter explores the multifaceted dimensions of Agile management and elucidates why its influence reaches far beyond the realm of project management.

- **Dynamic Adaptation to Change:** One of the foundational principles of Agile management is its inherent adaptability to change. While traditional project management often struggles with alterations in requirements, Agile thrives on them. The iterative and incremental nature of Agile methodologies allows organizations to respond swiftly to shifting market dynamics, customer expectations, and emerging opportunities. This dynamic adaptability is not restricted to project timelines but permeates the entire organizational ecosystem.

- **Cultural Transformation:** Agile is more than a set of methodologies; it instigates a profound cultural transformation within organizations. The Agile mindset prioritizes individuals and interactions over processes and tools, fostering a culture of collaboration, openness, and continuous improvement. This cultural shift is not confined to project teams but ripples through the entire organizational structure, influencing how teams collaborate, communicate, and innovate.

- **Stakeholder Engagement Beyond Projects:** Agile's emphasis on customer collaboration extends well beyond the boundaries of individual projects. It encompasses a holistic approach to stakeholder engagement, involving them in decision-making processes, product development, and strategic planning. By keeping stakeholders closely connected throughout the organizational journey, Agile ensures that the end results align with the evolving needs and expectations of all involved parties.

- **Agile Leadership and Strategic Agility:** Agile principles initially designed for project management have found a natural extension into leadership and strategic planning. Agile leadership is characterized by adaptability, responsiveness, and a willingness to embrace uncertainty. The iterative nature of Agile aligns seamlessly with strategic goals, transforming them from rigid plans into dynamic, responsive initiatives that can pivot in response to changing circumstances.

- **Continuous Improvement Across the Organization:** Agile transcends project boundaries by providing a framework for continuous improvement at an organizational scale. While Agile methodologies enhance project delivery through iterative cycles, organizations embracing Agile principles extend this philosophy to other business functions. Human resources, finance, marketing – all facets of an organization can benefit from the culture of continuous improvement that Agile instills.

Summary

In conclusion, Agile management emerges as a holistic philosophy that extends far beyond the realm of project management. Its impact touches every facet of an organization, fostering a culture of adaptability, collaboration, and continuous improvement. Recognizing Agile as a comprehensive management approach empowers organizations to navigate the complexities of the modern business landscape with resilience and innovation. Embracing Agile principles across all levels ensures that organizations not only deliver successful projects but also cultivate an environment conducive to sustained growth and success.

CHAPTER THIRTY-TWO

Understanding the Role of Agile Coach

Agile Coach in the modern Organizations

In an era characterized by rapid technological advancements and ever-changing market demands, organizations are increasingly adopting Agile methodologies to enhance their ability to adapt and deliver value efficiently. Central to the success of these Agile transformations is the role of an Agile Coach. In this chapter, we will explore the responsibilities, skills, and impact an Agile Coach has within modern organizations.

The Agile Paradigm

Agile methodologies, born out of the software development realm, have transcended their origins to become a philosophy guiding various facets of modern organizations. Agile emphasizes iterative development, collaboration, and customer feedback, fostering a culture of continuous improvement. However, successfully implementing Agile practices requires more than adopting a set of processes; it demands a cultural shift and a deep understanding of Agile principles.

The Role of an Agile Coach

An Agile Coach plays a pivotal role in guiding organizations through their Agile journey. The primary objective is to facilitate the adoption and consistent application of Agile practices, ensuring that teams and individuals embrace the Agile mindset.

Key aspects of the Agile Coach role:

- **Change Agent:** Agile Coaches act as change agents, catalyzing organizational transformation by instilling Agile values and principles at every level.

- **Guidance and Mentorship:** Provide guidance and mentorship to teams and individuals to help them understand and apply Agile methodologies effectively.

- **Facilitator of Agile Ceremonies:** Conduct and facilitate Agile ceremonies such as sprint planning, retrospectives, and daily stand-ups, ensuring they are conducted efficiently and effectively.

- **Continuous Improvement Advocate:** Foster a culture of continuous improvement by encouraging teams to reflect on their processes and outcomes and implement changes that enhance productivity and value delivery.

- **Collaboration Facilitator:** Promote cross-functional collaboration and communication, breaking down silos and fostering a shared sense of responsibility for project success.

- **Stakeholder Education:** Educate stakeholders at all levels about Agile principles and benefits, aligning their expectations with the iterative and adaptive nature of Agile methodologies.

- **Conflict Resolution:** Mediate conflicts and address impediments that hinder Agile adoption, ensuring a smooth and collaborative working environment.

- **Metrics and Feedback:** Establish relevant metrics to measure the success of Agile adoption, and provide constructive feedback to teams and individuals for continuous improvement.

Skills and Qualities of an Agile Coach

To be effective in their role, Agile Coaches need a diverse set of skills and qualities:

- **Deep Understanding of Agile:** Comprehensive knowledge of Agile frameworks, methodologies, and principles.

- **Communication Skills:** Excellent communication and interpersonal skills to effectively convey Agile concepts and principles to diverse audiences.

- **Adaptability:** The ability to adapt coaching approaches to suit the unique needs and challenges of different teams and organizational contexts.

- **Empathy:** A deep understanding of team dynamics and the ability to empathize with team members, fostering a positive and collaborative environment.

- **Leadership:** Strong leadership skills to inspire and motivate teams to embrace Agile values and practices.

- **Problem-Solving:** Effective problem-solving skills to address challenges and impediments hindering Agile adoption.

- **Continuous Learning:** A commitment to continuous learning and staying updated on evolving Agile practices and industry trends.

The Impact of Agile Coaches

The presence of skilled Agile Coaches can have a profound impact on modern organizations:

- **Increased Productivity:** Agile Coaches contribute to improved team efficiency and productivity by optimizing processes and promoting a focus on value delivery.

- **Enhanced Collaboration:** Fostering a collaborative culture, Agile Coaches break down communication barriers, leading to better cross-functional collaboration.

- **Adaptability and Resilience:** Teams coached by Agile Coaches become more adaptable, resilient, and responsive to change, crucial in today's fast-paced business environment.

- **Customer Satisfaction:** By emphasizing customer feedback and iterative development, Agile Coaches contribute to higher levels of customer satisfaction through the delivery of valuable, customer-centric products.

- **Cultural Transformation:** Agile Coaches play a key role in driving cultural transformation within organizations, aligning teams with the Agile mindset and principles.

Summary

In the ever-evolving landscape of modern organizations, the role of an Agile Coach is indispensable. Through their expertise, guidance, and advocacy for Agile principles, these professionals facilitate a cultural shift that enhances adaptability, collaboration, and value delivery. As organizations strive to stay competitive and responsive to market changes, the Agile Coach becomes a linchpin in their journey toward sustained success in an Agile world.

CHAPTER THIRTY-THREE

Applying Agile Management Beyond the IT Realm

Agile management, born out of the software development world, has transcended its IT origins to become a transformative force in various industries. Its principles, emphasizing adaptability, collaboration, and customer-centricity, have proven universally valuable. In this chapter, we explore the application of Agile management beyond IT, examining trends and success stories that showcase the versatility of Agile methodologies.

Agile in Marketing

- **Sprints and Iterations:** Traditional marketing often relies on long planning cycles. Agile principles introduce the concept of sprints and iterations, allowing marketing teams to adapt strategies quickly and respond to changing market dynamics.

- **Cross-functional Collaboration:** Agile encourages cross-functional collaboration, breaking down silos within marketing departments and fostering better communication between teams.

Agile Management in Various Sectors

- **Scalability:** Agile management methodologies like Scrum or Kanban offer scalability, allowing organizations to apply Agile principles to projects of all sizes and complexities.

- **Cross-functional Teams:** The success of Agile in project management lies in the formation of cross-functional teams that bring diverse skills and perspectives to the table.

Agile HR

- **Continuous Feedback:** Traditional annual performance reviews are being replaced by continuous feedback loops, aligning with Agile principles of regular assessment and improvement.

- **Agile Recruiting:** HR teams are adopting Agile practices in recruitment, shortening hiring cycles and adapting to changing talent requirements.

Agile Product Development in Non-Technical Fields

- **Prototyping and MVPs:** Beyond software, product development in industries like manufacturing and consumer goods benefits from Agile's emphasis on prototyping and minimum viable products (MVPs).

- **Customer Involvement:** Engaging customers early in the development process ensures that the final product meets their expectations and needs.

Agile Supply Chain Management

- **Responsive Supply Chains:** The dynamic nature of today's markets demands agile supply chain management. Organizations are reconfiguring their supply chains to be more responsive to changes in demand and disruptions.

- **Collaborative Networks:** Agile principles encourage collaboration among suppliers, manufacturers, and distributors to enhance overall supply chain efficiency.

Agile Healthcare

- **Iterative Protocols:** Healthcare institutions are adopting Agile methodologies in patient care, allowing for iterative protocols that can adapt to changing medical conditions.

- **Continuous Improvement:** An Agile mindset in healthcare promotes a culture of continuous improvement in processes, leading to better patient outcomes.

Agile Education

- **Adaptive Learning:** In education, Agile principles are transforming teaching methods. Adaptive learning programs tailor educational experiences based on continuous assessments and feedback.

- **Cross-functional Collaboration:** Schools and universities are breaking down departmental barriers, fostering collaboration between educators, administrators, and students.

Agile in Construction

- **Iterative Planning:** Construction projects, known for their complexity, benefit from Agile's iterative planning and scheduling, enabling teams to adapt to changes in project requirements.

- **Collaborative Teams:** Agile principles foster collaboration between architects, builders, and clients, resulting in more efficient and successful construction projects.

Agile in Finance

- **Iterative Budgeting:** Traditional budgeting can be rigid. Agile financial management introduces iterative budgeting, allowing organizations to adapt their financial plans based on changing business conditions.

- **Cross-functional Collaboration:** Collaboration between finance, operations, and other departments is crucial to achieving financial agility.

Agile in Retail

- **Adaptive Merchandising:** The retail sector is applying Agile principles to quickly adapt product offerings based on customer feedback and changing market trends.

- **Iterative Store Design:** Agile methodologies allow retailers to continuously optimize store layouts and designs based on customer behavior and preferences.

Summary

Agile management, once confined to IT, has evolved into a universal framework for driving innovation, collaboration, and adaptability across diverse industries. The trends discussed highlight the transformative impact of Agile principles, emphasizing the importance of agility in navigating the ever-evolving landscape of modern business. As organizations continue to embrace and adapt Agile methodologies, the journey beyond IT promises to be a dynamic and rewarding one, reshaping industries and fostering a culture of continuous improvement

CHAPTER THIRTY-FOUR

Transformation: Project Manager to Servant Leader

Transformation: Project Manager to Servant Leader

In the evolving landscape of project management, a transformative leadership style has gained prominence – Servant Leadership. For a traditional Project Manager, this shift represents not just a change in approach but a profound evolution in mindset and skills. This chapter explores how a Project Manager can attain the coveted skill of Servant Leadership and examines the multiple aspects that make this leadership style a powerful force in fostering team collaboration, empowerment, and overall project success.

Understanding Servant Leadership

Servant Leadership is a leadership philosophy that emphasizes the leader's role as a servant to their team. In contrast to traditional command-and-control styles, Servant Leadership focuses on serving the needs of others, enabling personal and professional growth, and fostering a collaborative and empowered team environment.

Empathy and Understanding

- **Traditional Approach:** Project Managers often focus on tasks, deadlines, and project outcomes. While these are essential, the human element is sometimes overlooked.

- **Servant Leadership Aspect:** Empathy is at the core of Servant Leadership. A leader who understands the aspirations, challenges, and emotions of team members can create a more supportive and inclusive work environment.

Leading by Example

- **Traditional Approach:** Project Managers may delegate tasks without actively participating in the day-to-day activities of the team.

- **Servant Leadership Aspect:** Servant Leaders lead by example, actively engaging in tasks alongside their team. This fosters a sense of unity, mutual respect, and shared commitment to project goals.

Facilitation of Growth and Development

- **Traditional Approach:** The focus may primarily be on getting the job done, with less emphasis on individual team member growth.

- **Servant Leadership Aspect:** Servant Leaders prioritize the growth and development of their team members. They provide mentorship, create opportunities for skill development, and support career advancement.

Fostering a Collaborative Culture

- **Traditional Approach:** Hierarchical structures can sometimes hinder open communication and collaboration.

- **Servant Leadership Aspect:** Servant Leaders actively promote a collaborative culture by encouraging open communication, valuing diverse perspectives, and creating a safe space for team members to voice their ideas and concerns.

Decision-Making through Consensus

- **Traditional Approach:** Decision-making may be centralized, with the Project Manager making most key decisions.

- **Servant Leadership Aspect:** Servant Leaders involve the team in the decision-making process, seeking consensus and valuing input from all members. This approach enhances team ownership and commitment.

Servant Leaders as Servants First

- **Traditional Approach:** Project Managers may see themselves as taskmasters or project drivers.

- **Servant Leadership Aspect:** Servant Leaders view themselves as servants first, focusing on meeting the needs of their team. This humble approach creates a positive and empowering work environment.

Servant Leaders as Enablers

- **Traditional Approach:** Project Managers may use command and control approach for providing specific instructions to the team.

- **Servant Leadership Aspect:** Servant Leaders enable the team by removing obstacles, providing resources, and empowering team members to take ownership of their work. This allows for a more self-directed and motivated team.

Promoting a Culture of Trust

- **Traditional Approach:** Trust may be based on positional authority than from the building of relationships.

- **Servant Leadership Aspect:** Servant Leaders build trust by being authentic, transparent, and consistently demonstrating a commitment to the team's well-being. Trust forms the foundation for effective collaboration and innovation.

Summary

The journey from a traditional Project Manager to a Servant Leader is a transformative process that requires a shift in mindset and a commitment to the well-being and growth of the team. By embracing empathy, leading by example, facilitating individual and collective growth, and fostering a collaborative culture, a Project Manager can evolve into a Servant Leader. In doing so, they not only enhance the project's chances of success but also contribute to a positive and empowering work environment where individuals can thrive, collaborate, and achieve their full potential. Servant Leadership is not just a skill to be acquired; it's a philosophy that can shape the trajectory of projects, products and the professional growth of the entire team.

CHAPTER THIRTY-FIVE

Epilogue: Reflections and Resolutions

The Summary

In the dynamic landscape of project management, the shift to Agile methodologies has become a cornerstone of success for organizations aiming to stay responsive and innovative. This book "Transforming Project Managers to Agile Roles" offers a comprehensive guide for project managers looking to make a seamless transition into pivotal roles such as Product Owner, Scrum Master, Change Agent, Program Manager, Servant Leader, and more. This transformative journey not only enhances individual careers but also positions professionals as catalysts for organizational agility.

- **Understanding the Agile Mindset:** At the core of this paradigm shift lies the Agile mindset - a commitment to adaptability, collaboration, and continuous improvement. The guide underscores the importance of internalizing these principles, laying the foundation for a cultural transformation within teams and organizations.

- **Demystifying Agile Roles:** The book provides a detailed exploration of various Agile roles, shedding light on the distinct responsibilities and skill sets required for each. From the visionary Product Owner aligning projects with customer needs to the facilitative Scrum Master guiding teams through iterative development, each role is dissected to offer a nuanced understanding.

Roles Explored:

- **Product Owner:** The visionary responsible for aligning project/product goals with customer needs.

- **Scrum Master:** The facilitator and coach, guiding teams through the Agile process.

- **Change Agent:** A catalyst for organizational transformation, driving a shift towards Agile practices.

- **Program Manager:** Orchestrating and synchronizing multiple Agile projects/ programs/ products to achieve strategic objectives.

- **Servant Leader:** Committed to serving the team, removing impediments, and fostering self-organization.

Strategies for Transition:

The guide offers practical strategies for project managers to acquire the necessary skills and mindset for Agile roles. This includes recommendations for training, exploring, and experiential learning opportunities. Additionally, it addresses common challenges faced during the transition, such as overcoming resistance to change and navigating organizational inertia.

Benefits and Opportunities:

The book highlights the tangible benefits of embracing Agile methodologies, such as fostering innovation, enhancing team collaboration, and delivering customer value. It emphasizes how Agile roles not only represent a career evolution but also empower individuals to become leaders in driving organizational success in today's fast-paced business environment.

We have explored the transformative power of Agile Management in today's dynamic and fast-paced business landscape. Traditional managerial approaches, once effective in stable environments, now face the challenge of keeping up with the demands of constant change and innovation. The shift to Agile Management is not merely a trend but a necessity, as it aligns leaders with the principles of adaptability, collaboration, and customer-centricity. Embracing an Agile mindset allows managers to navigate uncertainty with flexibility, respond to evolving market dynamics, and foster a culture of continuous improvement. In the pursuit of organizational resilience and success, this shift from traditional to Agile roles becomes not just a choice but a strategic imperative for those at the helm of steering their teams through the complexities of the modern business landscape. This book serves as a compass, navigating professionals through the transformative journey of adopting Agile roles and positioning themselves as integral players in modern management within forward-thinking organizations.